A HANDFUL OF BEADS

Jean Meade-Fetherstonhaugh

A Handful of Beads

JEAN MEADE-FETHERSTONHAUGH

SERENDIPITY

People travel to wonder the height of mountains, at the huge waves of the sea, at the long courses of rivers, at the vast compass of the ocean, at the circular motion of the stars, and they pass by themselves without wondering.

St Augustine

THE FOLLOWING STORY is like a string of beads, representing all the small miracles which have amounted to my life.

Some of the beads are beautiful, shining and bright. Some are of wonderful, jewel-like colours; some are clouded, dark and heavy. Some are very valuable materially, some are of value because of their vibration, as these beads, like different crystals, have different energies.

Some of them inevitably are flawed, but I have strung all of them on a thread to make a whole, not yet complete, necklace. The thread holding them together has been my faith in God, (or if no God, in Apex Mentis written on the apex of the pyramid, meaning the 'heart of mind' consciousness). Sometimes, the thread has got tangled, sometimes a bit thin, but always strong enough to bear the beads.

Without the string, the handful of beads would have little meaning. One of the strands of the string was made of the gift of healing, which many of us are given, like the gift of being musical or artistic, and which develops if we appreciate and use it. One of the vital beads was the question, 'why am I here?' The pearls are my family.

I hope this endeavour may try to answer this, on many different levels. There have always been little miracles bringing to me a teacher at the right time. So many wonderful people have helped me thread the beads – too many to enumerate, but each has given me some very valuable part of the whole

– to them all, I can only say Thank-you for helping me to keep going. I would especially like to thank David Tredinnick MP for helping me over the last fence. Thank-you to Carmen Fernandez who came into my life at exactly the right time to give me healing, courage, enthusiasm and her expertise in typing my illegible muddle; and also to Phyllis Kenney and Liz Tansley. I hope in some way readers will be able to add some beads to their own necklaces having read this book.

Contents

Foreword

Teresa Hale

TWENTY-FIVE YEARS AGO, I had this dream that I wanted to bring orthodox and complementary medicine together under one roof where practitioners of different disciplines could work together. I saw medicine as an art as well as a science, which could combine compassion with rigour, and true healing involving the body, mind and spirit.

This dream became a reality and The Hale Clinic is now seen as an institution for the expression of these values, as well as a model for others wishing to open similar clinics.

Whenever a vision is realised, it is so important to honour and remember the people who were there before us. They were the early pioneers who laid their foundations for a wider acceptance of spirituality, healing and complementary medicine today. They held the dream together when these ideas were not widely accepted. Like beacons of light they showed us the way and gave us the strength and confidence to face the challenges ahead.

Like George Trevelyan and Wellsley Tudor Pole, Jean Meade-Fetherstonhaugh was one of those pioneering lights. Her enthusiasm and absolute confidence in healing and spirituality were a great source of encouragement to me.

Jean Meade-Fetherstonhaugh, by being both a part of the British establishment and a healer, was a living example of how these ideas could be integrated into mainstream society. Her example strengthened my own resolve that this was possible.

I will always remember spending inspirational weekends with Jean and will always be grateful for her unending support and belief in my vision.

Teresa Hale

David Harvey

IN 1983, DAVID HARVEY PUBLISHED a book called *The Power to Heal* in which he reports of the ability of one individual to heal another through touch alone which spans the centuries from before the time of Hippocrates to the present day; yet what must rate as one of Man's most precious resources has been surpassed, ignored and even discredited until recently.

Now the ability to heal, described by one scientist as 'the best kept secret of the Millennium', is being rediscovered. This fascinating and timeless book reveals the inside story of healing, and its author dedicated it thus:

> I cannot help but mention one person in particular, to whom I owe a rather special debt. It was Jean Meade who made me realise the scope and potential of healing, and introduced me to new worlds, which I am still exploring. To Jean, my first teacher – I shall be for ever grateful.

This inspiring memoir for the New Millennium is Jean Meade's own story of an integrated life as a traveller on the path...

CHAPTER ONE

Stepping Stones to a New Awareness

Childhood – Galloway – Granny – Convent school religion – Paris – War

I WAS BORN ON 8 March 1921, so I am under the sign of Pisces, with Aquarius rising, and astrologers tell me there is a great deal of water in my chart and little air. Water is spirituality, sensitivity, intuition and the imagination. Air unfortunately as far as I understand means the intellect so this didn't seem to augur very well, but I've had a very interesting and varied life and I will record bits and pieces that I remember.

My first memory of anything must have been when I was under two and is one of great sadness. My father owned a most wonderful dog. He

Galloway – Southwest Scotland

Jean

bought her from the gypsies and she was called Vim. She was a wolf-hound brindle in colour like a whippet with enormously long legs. She was a very gentle dog and I remember really loving her very much. One day, she produced puppies, and to my absolute delight I was given one.

Then a rather terrifying grown-up came to stay who was my paternal grandmother. I always had a feeling of dislike towards her and imagined when I was small that it was because she always had a drip on her nose, but in fact not so many years ago my mother told me that she used to drink – it's very interesting that children always instinctively know if an adult is off balance in some way. They sometimes don't particularly mind, but I think they avoid people who are off balance without of course having any idea why.

Anyway, I remember being on the floor playing with the puppy and this rather sinister voice saying to someone else way above my head: 'That child is far too small to have a puppy,' and the puppy subsequently disappeared. I remember experiencing the most awful, painful, emotional grief. Of course, it didn't last at all. A child's grief, as long as the child has a loving and supportive home, seems to pass, whereas that of an adult can last for the rest of his or her lifetime. It must surely be better to express grief, as in eastern cultures – to beat the breast, tear the clothes, wail and express it all openly and publicly – than allow life to go on as it should. Once grief has been expressed outwardly, it seems to heal like a wound. A child without inhibitions or conditioning does just this. This feeling of sadness is like a wave that gathers up the emotion of the moment from the heart and swells to become a crest which breaks to pass away back into the sea. If only as we grew up we could remember this and simply accept the feelings of both sadness and gladness and go with them until the wave breaks then let go, our faith would remain intact throughout our lives. Instead, many people hold onto sadness and suffer. Accept and you will be free. Jesus often taught that we should be like a child, and a child if allowed suffers sadness only at the time and then grows into the next moment – in the same way children should be allowed to accept death.

Then I don't remember anything much until quite a few years later. I remember an experience I had, being taken to the sea with my younger sisters, with a nanny. It was a great joy and a delight because I was free to give way to my imagination like all children at the sea. It was fashionable in those days to send children to Frinton-on-Sea.

I remember endless paddling and shrimping, and building one's ideas in sand. I remember wearing a very painful garment which was a kind of pantaloon with a pinafore front, with elastic around the top of the leg. My earliest recollection of the sea seems to be associated with the feeling of wet sand rubbing round the top of one's legs, and a sun bonnet with the wet frill around the neck flapping in one's face. I suppose the weather must have been different then, in fact hot in summer, cold in winter.

The best and most enchanted years of my childhood were spent when we moved near Gatehouse of Fleet, a beautiful place in Galloway in south west Scotland, where my father had an immense sheep farm going on up into wonderful hills – this place was a child's paradise, wonderful burns trickling down where you could make pools and dam them up with stones, heather where you could hide, every possible scope for imagination, and I think I always had a great imagination. I never remember being without companions, imaginary or real, in the shape of two younger sisters, Audrey and Susan, but my imaginary companions were far more enjoyable.

Indeed, I always felt that there were fairies about and I had great communication with them.

How do adults ever really know if children actually do see something when they say they see fairies that have manifested to them? A child probably has not entirely lost the use of inner sight and hearing, and I do really believe that some children see or realise something which is an extension of what we adults call 'normal', a seeing of other dimensions. I experienced the same thing when I was doing a lot of healing, as I was then constantly tuned in to this inner seeing. One of the first people who came for healing had a head problem, and so I had placed my hands on their head, and all of a sudden I found myself (I thought) floating above them near the ceiling of a high room looking down on the scene. When I saw astronauts in flight, I imagined they must feel like this too – out of one's body, yet absolutely ordinary in mind.

We lived in a lovely house called Murrayton, very high up on a hill.

Every day we were sent out for a walk with whoever was looking after us. We very often had Swiss au pair girls, which was when I began speaking French, and we always had to walk down to the bottom of the hill and get our fairy bicycles out of the shed before we started off in any direction at all, but this was a time of wonderful fun. The small burns in which I and my siblings used to fish for brown trout ran down past our house on the hill and grew to quite a big river at the bottom. This was a constant source of delight and it was strewn along its banks and river bed with a wonderful assortment of granite stones which were very sparkly. They must have had a good deal of quartz crystal in them, and it was extraordinary that even then I had a real obsession about collecting the most sparkling of these granite stones containing quartz. I now work with precious stones and crystals and know their power and magic.

There were wonderful days when we were allowed to go off, the three of us on our own with a terrier. The terrier caught a rabbit and I remember skinning and gutting the rabbit thinking nothing of it, because I was very well taught by my father to do a great many practical things. We built enormous and wonderful bonfires over which we roasted it for our lunch. Interestingly, I later realised my father must have been a powerful healer – not only was he a magician with horses which he trained but with any wild animal which would not go near anyone else. He charmed them. They felt his magnetism – and though normally he was unapproachable and non-communicative, when I was ill he would come and put his hands on me and a feeling of light, peace and utter bliss would come over me. The word healer at that time was certainly never mentioned nor talked about though it existed before time began.

I became intrigued by all the edible berries and leaves that I found – after boiling them up over a bonfire then consuming them. Even then it seems I had a natural inclination for herbs and herbal medicine without any knowledge. Sometimes this led to a tummy ache – but luckily never worse. This interest developed into my becoming an obsessive gardener, mainly of herbs and vegetables. I have always managed to make a garden and grow herbs for my own use wherever I have lived. Even nursing in the war we had tomatoes outside the operating theatre, where they thrived on blood.

Every day, one of my two sisters had to take turns with me to walk over the hill with a can to fetch milk from our shepherd's house. It was some miles, and a weary job, but greatly rewarded by the Scottish hospitality awaiting us. It is the custom in Scotland always to offer a 'piece', which could be anything from a scone to a huge meal. We always had a scone, and there were lots of different kinds – soda scones, drop scones, treacle scones, oatcakes and more. I was very greedy, and it kept my legs from aching too much. This hospitality is often the custom in Ireland too, certainly in Middle Eastern countries among Arab people, travellers, nomads, and in Spain. It seems only the English are too introverted to share this custom, or is it that people are unconscious of the vital importance of sharing?

I met Mother Theresa once for a brief moment years later. At the time I was starting a healing centre at St James's Church, Piccadilly, and she had come to speak in England and Ireland. I was amazed to meet such a tiny, rather wizened, crumpled up Saint, wrapped in white with blue headband and sandals. She emanated compassion. She told a story of how surrounded by starving children she had pulled a crust from her pocket and put it into the hand of a small boy. Instead of wolfing it down, he broke a small part and put it in his mouth – the rest into a small bag. When she asked him why he hadn't eaten it, he said: 'The rest is for my brothers and sisters. We share.' This was a gesture made by a child at starvation level. Sharing is part of compassion, and should be part of our very nature. Some cultures who live a life on the move in tents have no store houses, and all share what they have, however small. Everyone has a part of the joy of whatever is shared, and all the great teachings tell us to share – shared prayer, shared feasts, shared grief, even – benefits all who are participating.

I remember sometimes dressing up as Red Indians with real feather head-dresses. Of course I didn't know at that time that Native Americans used the feathers in their head-dresses to show stages of initiations – the chief therefore would have had a complete display – others had fewer feathers until more were merited. We each of us had what we called our house, which was a sort of cave house built in the middle of the most enormous pile of wood which had been cut down to clear the bank of the river. I used to spend a great deal of time picking through our rubbish to collect tin cans and all kinds of goodies which I took to my house. We also had doll's houses and these were a constant source of interest and enterprise because they were made out of fruit boxes and all the furniture had to be devised and made by whichever one of us could think up something. Lots of beautiful furniture was created from matchboxes and reels of cotton and little bits and pieces. I think it's really sad that children nowadays have the most beautiful ready-made doll's houses bought for them and they don't experience the great satisfaction and joy of what later turns into job satisfaction. If you have to think up what you're going to make, make your own blueprint, collect the bits and pieces and by sheer ingenuity put them together to create something pleasing to yourself, it really is far more satisfying than anything that is just produced ready-made. Time is the factor that we always have to deal with and time now for young parents takes on quite a different priority to what it did in the days when I was young.

My dolls house had a family and this family really took almost precedence in all my thoughts. For a very long time there were Mr and Mrs Brown and two children. I'm sure modern psychologists would have some amazing explanation for this but I haven't been into it and I don't know what it would be, but Mr and Mrs Brown and their two children were very important to me and I never went anywhere without them. They lived in my pockets and they also came in a toy car I had whenever we went on our fairly rare family outings. I must have been a very boring child for my parents because either one of the Brown children had fallen out somewhere and our steps had to be retraced or there was some drama over my family and they had been forgotten and we had to go back and get them. However, they survived a great many years.

I remember a wonderful episode when I had a friend to stay who was my age and together we found and enlarged a huge cave in the garden in some rocks. We were given an old bearskin rug which we took in turns to wear, imagining ourselves as ancient Britons. We kept the most extraordinary animals in boxes; I can't think how they survived – they probably didn't for more than a few days. Some entailed grubbing for worms to feed them on. Another time from somewhere we captured some bats. I think they proved to be rather dull and probably didn't stay very long either.

The boy I played with rose to great heights, and is now a very important person in the business world. He hadn't, through the years, always enjoy the reminiscences about this particular time in his life, though we always remained very good friends.

The most wonderful of all our outings was when we were taken a few miles to the sea near Gatehouse, our nearest town. The sea, which was my idea of heaven, was especially beautiful on the Galloway coast. Completely unknown, untouched, unspoilt – the pine trees and heather grew right down to the shore where there were miles and miles of silver sand thickly overlaid with exquisite shells of hundreds of different kinds.

This enabled hours of collecting – what a choice there was. The tide would go out for miles leaving endless rock pools and islands. One large island on which there were rocks, trees and heather would be completely surrounded at high tide. I always had a private, secret world and liked to be alone. I walked onto the island at low tide and hid in a crack in the rocks. To my joy I realised that if I stayed quiet, no-one would find me, the tide would come in and I would be alone and isolated. I must have overlooked the practical facts, apart from my parents' worry, about no food nor water for twelve hours. However, this was not to be – somehow my by now demented mother realised where I might be and with shouted threats I was persuaded to come out and wade to the shore before high tide. But the sea has drawn me all my life – water and the feeling of endless space – looking out to the light which is always there enhancing my visions – and which has no end. The sound of the sea is soothing and exciting – bigger and more powerful than anything human. It is also frightening but a recognisable form of fear.

I love swimming – and I always recapture this feeling of complete freedom and being detached which I first had during those expeditions to the sea at Gatehouse. All my life I have wanted to be near the sea. I remember very few moments of distress during this period of my life, but I do remember being slightly overawed when there was a great fire in the hills. From time to time, sparks flew out of the train. The railway line ran through the hills, and if the heather was very dry it caught fire and there were devastating fires for miles, which meant that my father and any shepherds or anyone living within any possible range got together and went up to beat out the fires with great flat twig brushes. I remember seeing my father come in blackened and exhausted; obviously there was a great worry because at one time a great fire came within a field of our house. But again in a childish way one remembers these things briefly and it passed like the wind.

Jim was my best and only friend. He was one of our shepherd's sons, my age, and he was a wonderful companion; good, honest as daylight, fun, full of laughter, and he went along with all my imaginary games. He taught me so much country lore – how to tickle trout for hours with our hands in the bubbling brown burn until our fingers could creep under the trout lying there and grab them under the gills to bring them out, if lucky, triumphant. He taught me how to corner a sheep and catch it with the handle of a crook, which all shepherds carried, how to skin rabbits, how to salt and cure moleskins. I was always aiming at a fur coat but alas, my childish impatience always prevented this. The big thrill was to go ferreting, muzzling the ferrets and putting them down a rabbit-hole hoping they would flush out rabbits to be caught in the net placed over the other burrows. Then slowly my friendship with Jim began to change as we both grew up and became self-conscious – but here was someone who really lived according to the laws of the cosmos and therefore lived a hard but completely harmonious life. Growing up presented no problems to him.

Jim often came to tea but it was far more rewarding to go to tea in his cottage. Tea with any of the shepherds was a great treat – there were always lots of different scones and jams and shortbread, and there was no restriction either on how much one could eat. Being a very greedy child this was part of the treat. Jim's family lived away up in the hills near a Roman viaduct over a river. He also had smaller brothers and sisters, two were twins. One awful day I was told the news. Jim's smaller brother had put the twins in the river to see if they would float – they sank – this was a terrible sadness. There were also wonderful happy gatherings when all the shepherds from farms miles around met together to clip the sheep, moving from farm to farm as a communal enterprise. How sad that this spirit of sharing seems no longer to exist. The clipping of course took probably a day or two – the great feast at lunchtime made up for the hard walk over the hills to get there. Once a year the sheep were gathered off the hills and herded into pens where they were put through a sheep dip and marked red to check they'd been done. This was a rather sadistic pleasure to be allowed to watch – exciting as the sheep protested and awful as they were pushed under this peculiar smelling dip – sometimes the privilege was accorded to us to shut or open the gate of the pen. My father used to shout a lot and was rather frightening, but it was exciting nevertheless.

Suddenly, things changed. I supposed my mother realised I was growing up. One day she called me into the drawing room and told me I would no longer do the things I'd done with Jim, nor could he spend time playing with us all in our house. I suppose this was trying to teach me all about social separation as it was in those days. This was a most devastating, shattering blow. There did not appear to be any explanation and I don't think I ever asked for one. I dumbly accepted. Of course, I went on playing with Jim, but anyway we were growing away from each other and Jim began to work, though I did feel sad.

Another big thrill was the weekly arrival at the top of the hill of the VAN. The van was a kind of mini-superstore – it stocked everything. The first shoppers allowed on were my mother and our cook, who bought for the week. Then at last, I and my sisters were allowed on to spend our pocket money, sixpence! This enjoyable pastime could last hours, people had more patience and time then. Lots of small bags of sweets were chosen and purchased, and secretly initiated by Jim, a packet of Wills Woodbines. These were the cheapest cigarettes, made, we had heard, out of tobacco sweepings. Next came the fearful experiment with Jim of lighting up and smoking one of these fags down a rabbit-hole in case of fire in the heather as we were well-hidden. Then the awful realisation that my mouth and lungs were full of smoke, the taste was disgusting and to my horror I felt sick – what an anticlimax to the end of a daring adventure.

Sometimes we went on fairy bikes, which were kept in a hut at the bottom of the hill, to visit my Aunt Helen Murray-Baillie who lived in a large house, down the valley, called Castramont. Built on a Roman ruin which was once a castle, it always gave me fanciful ideas of living in a castle myself. I discovered later in life that Alice Bailey, the great theosophist, lived here in her childhood. Aunt Helen was a very dignified, formidable and eccentric lady. A relation of my father, she had lived much of her life in Italy, where she had led a cultured and elegant life. She later built herself a replica of her Italian house in Gatehouse. An enormous part of the land in Galloway once belonged to my father's relations and to Aunt Helen's daughter (my father's cousin). Aunt Helen had beautiful chattels, furniture and pictures, a fabulous garden as the climate was part of the Gulf Stream, and superb food. She was terrifying as she wore a lorgnette and when one was speaking, or worse, eating, she would put up her lorgnettes and bend from a great height to have a good look. I felt permanently under scrutiny.

I was transported once a week down the hill in McMurray's sidecar, equivalent of a local taxi, a motorbike with a sidecar that bounced about as it went – McMurray wore goggles and long leather gloves. He also kept the watch and jewellery shop in Gatehouse. I was left at Aunt Helen's for the day to learn culture. We had French lessons, she was very severe, French reading, history and mythology. She also taught me about her Chinese Chippendale furniture and porcelain. I was always terrorised, and have disliked Chinese chattels ever since, but I did learn. Little did I know how useful Aunt Helen's education would be later in life when I lived at Uppark. The lunch was my only joy – delicious food served by her butler – no second helpings allowed, and she always scrutinised one's plate just to see how much I had taken.

She rode a large white horse side-saddle and once turned up at Murrayton in voluminous pink bloomers and boots and a large, wide brimmed hat with ostrich feathers in it! I only remember one occasion when we had to dress up. It was for a very big wedding. My cousin Betty was to marry and I and my sisters were bridesmaids. We had red velvet dresses and gold wreaths on our heads. I loved the dress and had it for years though I hardly had occasion to wear it. I think the only time I had been to church was when we stayed with my grandparents in the south at Welton at Christmas so this was a big thrill – a wedding in the local town in Gatehouse. We were all assembled and the wedding began. I stood staring and waiting, endlessly waiting, for it to begin. The bride arrived and walked to join her husband at the end of the church where there was a table and beside it a fiddler. Prayers began. I still waited – after a while the fiddler played and the married couple turned round and came away. I was still waiting for what I imagined was going to happen. I'd thought that the end wall would open to show an altar with candles and a screen and the wedding would then begin. I had never been to a Scottish church, or kirk, where this doesn't happen. I was dismayed and quite troubled – subsequently asking many questions about the strange service, which went unanswered. It was the first time I had thought about religion and quite a shock. We piled into my Aunt Helen's Rolls Royce and were driving through the streets lined with locals as my family were well-known lairds, when Aunt Helen leant over me, tapping my shoulder with her lorgnette and said, 'Wave, dear, wave,' as if we were royalty. People were treated like that in those old-fashioned days but I was most impressed – a funny occasion.

My parents took it in turns to teach us, having had about fifteen unsuccessful governesses within a few years – they taught such things as they were able and had time for. My mother taught us lovely things, read us stories, sang to us and taught history. My father undertook an uphill task which always ended in a deadlock – teaching me mathematics. Oh the tears, the fears, the agony. I have never learned mathematics. I was so afraid of my father that I used to say yes I understood when I perfectly well didn't. It's terrible how people through fear do very strange things. I used to lie like a trooper too, and a lot of my lying was because I had this tremendous imagination, dare one call it that? I never know now whether things existed in my imagination, or if they were real. There is a very thin line between the two. I lived with imaginary or visionary little people, I knew them well, I had conversations with them, it was a world really that I inhabited much more than the world of reality. My mother, who is now ninety-two told me not so long ago that when I was thirteen, if she had been able to afford it, she would have taken me to a psychiatrist because of these people I lived with, luckily however, no such thing happened. The people and the imaginary world faded up to a point, but it is difficult, if a child sees and hears on the two sense levels which adults have lost the use of, and is always told, even punished, for imagining or lying or inventing. It will inevitably, usually at about the age when it goes to school, seven, eight or nine, realise that there really is a sort of dual aspect of things and the aspect that adults can't feel, hear or understand is best kept a secret.

It was about this time, I suppose I must have been about nine or ten, that my father took me out on one of the many expeditions rounding up sheep into the hills, and on the expedition he taught me to dowse for water using a split hazel stick. It is very curious that I don't remember any sense of excitement or any sense of the extraordinary; I simply took it for granted, and it worked for me.

But very much later in retrospect I realised that I had kept this particular faculty a secret; not consciously kept as a secret but simply never talked about it or used it until some long time later, well, certainly years later, when healing, when I found that this current of cosmic energy sent through my hands could be directed to various uses, though it took me half a lifetime to realise I could use it in response to a burning desire to use my hands to help sick people.

So in childhood I had first felt the desire to look after sick things, and I suppose it was at this time that I began to think about wanting to be a doctor, for which I certainly never would have been clever enough. Meanwhile the only possible patient was a perfectly disgusting rabbit which had myxomatosis. I remember my mother's absolute horror when she discovered a half dead, or maybe even dead, rabbit being nursed in the doll's pram; it had obviously been there for several days, which was rather unfortunate. I also remember various moles and even bats being nurtured for a while until they were discovered, or possibly recovered and went away, or died.

We were all allowed to keep animals which was good, things like mice, rabbits and guinea-pigs. I had mice. I remember this being the most immense excitement and really the beginning of learning about life, also responsibility, traumatic to a degree when I had some white mice in a nice large cage with a glass front. I remember it well. They were kept in an outside laundry. There came the day when the mice had babies, tremendously exciting, lots and lots of them. But when the novelty of this wore off, I suppose I was distracted and had ideas and thoughts about other things and for several days on end I forgot to feed them. When I went to see the mice, what did I see? There had been total carnage, they had been cannibals, only one large mouse left and half a dead body; this made the most horrific impression that is so clear now, probably as clear as at the time the horror swept over me. My immediate reaction was my absolute terror at having to admit to my parents that I had killed all my mice, worse, starved them to death. I remember spending the whole day hiding before I dared own up in a very roundabout way to my poor mother, who I presume had to deal with the situation because I did not dare to go, not only in the laundry but anywhere near it for weeks and weeks on end; however, no doubt it was probably quickly forgotten.

I then had guinea-pigs – two who multiplied to twenty-two – I taught them to follow me in the woods and kept them in a dog kennel – until another drama – the rats got in and killed all but one, and I wept over their deaths for a long time.

The highlight of the year was a visit south for Christmas to stay with my maternal grandparents – the Garrards. They lived in a large, beautiful house and village called Welton in Northamptonshire. My grandfather Harry Garrard was descended from a well-known line of craftsmen. Garrards from the eighteenth century were goldsmiths, silversmiths, bronze-casters, painters and the crown jewellers. My grandfather received and looked after three generations of royalty in his establishment at Albermarle Street, London. They came to choose jewellery and refit their crowns – or in the case of Princess Elizabeth and Princess Margaret, as they were then, to have them made. As Garrards were the crown jewellers they had the task of making small crowns at the time of the coronation of King George VI for the two princesses. On one visit my grandfather's manager wanted model heads to try them on, so whose better than ours? My head was too large, but my smaller cousin obliged. I remember how beautiful the work in them was, and the meticulous craftsmanship which was carried out. Many other crowns of English and foreign royalty were cared for by Garrards until years after my grandfather was dead with no male successor, the business was sold to other jewellers but still bears the name Garrard. My grandmother's family were descended from Cazenoves – French Huguenots. Garrards made the finest precision tools in Europe, and also clocks and watches in works in Swindon. My grandfather travelled to his works in both places by coach. His coaching timetable still exists and the journey took not much longer than the present railways.

Welton was in the middle of the best hunting country – the Pytchley – and my parents came south to hunt – my father a superb horseman, looking impressive in red coat and top hat, my mother in black habit, riding side-saddle as ladies did in those days. Everyone seemed to hunt – the doctor, the vicar, the local bank manager, most of the farmers and anyone else with a horse. People all seemed so happy to be enjoying a day's sport together. Later I was taught to ride but did not really enjoy it much and was too fearful to enjoy hunting.

The journey south was a big move and we looked forward to it for months. It was such an excitement and such a big movement, because we had to go by train from our local station, up in the hills, eight miles from the small town. There the train was especially stopped to pick us up with whoever was travelling with us. Not only were we three small girls but we had a mass of animals. At one time, we had mice in a cage, presumably in a small box for travelling, a canary in a cage and one terrible time for the grown-ups was when I had a ferret. But anyway all these things had to come with us and go up in the rack of the carriage and away we went for this thrilling journey over the viaduct. This was a Roman viaduct, which still exists though I don't think the railway still works over it. This was at the end of our sheep farm and was near the border into England. We arrived at Carlisle where we were met, believe it or not, by the stationmaster in person. This obviously had been laid on, but he was always a sort of safety landmark wearing a top hat and a frock coat. So the local train disgorged this party who were taken care of by the stationmaster and presumably put on the express train south for Rugby, our destination. There we were met by our grandmother's chauffeur in a very large car which again was hugely exciting. I seem to remember a look of some disdain on the chauffeur's face which I'm sure I noticed because it was a look I didn't recognise. I couldn't understand why everybody shouldn't simply love to see us and all our animals, varied as they were in cages. I do of course absolutely see his point now.

What fun it was being with all our cousins all together in this huge lovely house. We were up on the top floor in what I suppose one would call the attic. I am sure that the room we were left to sleep in must have been haunted but never, subsequently, has there been any knowledge or mention of any possibility of this. Maybe I was just a very over-imaginative child but the nights were a horror to me; from the moment the light went out, I imagined dark figures prowling, particularly coming out from under the bed. Apart from that, the days were one long constant delight because I adored my Granny.

Granny talked about God, describing him as omnipotent awesome with a long white beard sitting on a golden throne crowned with jewels, as seen in Victorian pictures. I didn't like the sound of this much, and I didn't think about God again for years. When Granny was very old and wandering, she was very afraid to die because of her idea of God. How sad that in the Victorian era, religion was so dictatorial, dogmatic, a gloomy myth. Granny was such a very good person, such a very good listener, such a kind person, indeed she indulged absolutely everybody she ever met. We were often indulged with being allowed one sweet after lunch, but Granny always managed to smuggle several more into both pockets of one's coat. There were always lovely little extras from Granny. I was a very greedy child, and I remember at meals in the dining room all the grandchildren had a table at the side and on the sideboard there would be several dishes each containing some delightful food but we were only allowed one thing, and so Granny used to come creeping up. She had a wonderful way of compromising that if you had a very little of the one thing, you could have lots of little bits of all the others. Constant delight – I was really very greedy – my grandchildren simply delight in the story of how when I was very first allowed to sit at the grown-up table we had a wonderful fruit salad and I had decided that the best thing in the fruit salad was the cherry which I left on the side of my plate. I had nearly finished the rest of my fruit salad when to my absolute horror a grown-up's fork leant over my plate and spiked off the cherry. It was actually a very funny joke but I remember my utter dismay and horror at the time. This obviously stuck because it's a story, as I said, that my grandchildren simply adore hearing still, over and over – never leave the best bit till last.

My grandparents' house was in the middle of a village which was built on a very steep hill. The house and a very big garden and park were in the middle of it, so any expedition outside the walls of the garden involved either going up or down. 'Mrs' was my grandfather's coachman's wife and when my mother and her sisters were small, the coachman always talked about her as The Mrs so it was presumed that her name was Mrs, and Mrs, she was always known as. She was the most wonderful character who knew everyone's sorrows and joys and shared everything with the family. She was enormous, always dressed in black bombazine with a million small buttons up the front of her dress and a little black stand-up collar with a lace frill around the inside. When Mrs went out on a shopping expedition she wore the most beautiful bonnets. I remember a most wonderful black bonnet with a huge black satin bow under her chin and some black ostrich feathers at the side, absolutely bewitching. The treat when going to tea with Mrs was to be allowed to wash up what was obviously her most treasured tea set in her sink, which was a stone sink. To get the water you had to hand pump it from an outside well, cold of course; the excitement was intense.

At this very early age, my grandmother taught us to be aware of making some contribution outside the family and into the village, the community, the town or wherever we lived. I remember my grandmother sending us each afternoon on a walk and always at the beginning we had to take something like a rice pudding to various people in the village. This was a hazard. Up the hill in one house there was a very old lady called Mrs Porter of whom we were absolutely terrified. She really was the personification of a witch, certainly to look at because she lived her life in a tall winged armchair with her back to the light, with a black shawl around her shoulders. Poor Mrs Porter in fact was absolutely totally deaf and she made the most horrible screeching animal sounds, which honestly to a small child were completely terrifying. As we approached with the rice pudding, she used to put out her claw-like hands and hold one's arm and then demand to be kissed. It really was a dreaded visit, but anyway we had to learn to take the rough with the smooth. There was another more enchanting person who lived down the bottom of the village called Mrs Cartwright who was fascinating to us because she had fourteen children. There came the day when one of the children, a boy in his teens, came running up the village with his fingers hanging, several chopped off in the machine that was chopping manglewurzel. He arrived at the back door of the great house where he was swept into the servants' hall. By this time whoever was looking after us had also gone to see what was happening. So we were abandoned, naturally we had a whiff of what was going on but we didn't dare enter forbidden territory, which was downstairs in the servants' hall. So I remember madly piling boxes one on the other in order to get a good view through a rather high up window. I can't remember actually seeing anything, but it was dramatic and for us rather exciting. I suppose in due course the young man was taken off by the chauffeur to the local hospital. I don't know how the story ended, I hope as well as possible. No NHS in those days, but people seemed more compassionate and charitable to me.

Another expedition when staying with Granny was to be allowed to go up to the village to buy sweets. There were two sweet shops. One we simply adored, it was kept by a scruffy old woman named Mrs Lyman who always had a dripping nose, a hacking cough and masses and masses of children who sat outside her sweetie shop on the pavement eating bread and jam. Naturally I envied them terribly. But Mrs Lyman had lots and lots of very cheap sweets in boot boxes, highly coloured, which were served in the most wonderful three-cornered paper bags. She didn't ever mind how many different lots we had, and somehow one always seemed to get an enormous number for a very small amount of money. The sweet shop we were really supposed to go to was kept a bit further up the road by a very genteel lady called Katie. She was terribly nice but her sweets were far less accessible; they were kept in enormous glass jars in rows along the back of the shop and the agony was one had to make up one's mind which you wanted without having little tastes. However, sometimes we had to patronise her shop as well.

When we were not allowed to go into the village I became adventure-some. There was a very large garden – part of which was a rose garden, mysterious because it was surrounded by high clipped yew hedges and it was forbidden. In the middle was a bench and once I learnt to read I saw it said, 'One is nearer God's heart in a garden than anywhere else on earth' – I think curiosity spurred me on to learn to read more. I have frequently quoted this verse in all my various gardens. However, greatly daring I went into the rose garden and at one end it had a door. The door opened directly on to the village street quite near the sweet shop. So with a short dash Mrs Lyman's sweet shop would be reached and a purchase risked.

I remember Granny also taking me on an expedition to the workhouse in Daventry. This was really rather a horror, but I suppose as a child you couldn't relate other awful circumstances to your own – somehow it remained remote and I can't remember having any particular impression of it, except the sorrow when Granny explained that people went into the workhouse for a bath, bed and breakfast, then were turned out for the day – locked out, in fact. This was long before the social services were in action, but there were very fewer people needing this kind of help. Granny taught me not only to take from society but to give back, and to have an interest in other people's lives – she enthused me with a desire to help people.

One day she took me with her, driven by the chauffeur, to London to visit the slums. This was a fantastic eye-opener to me. There we were in narrow streets full of rubbish, amongst minute, filthy houses out of which poured children in rags, with no shoes and sores on their faces and runny noses. I felt an awful blackness descend on me like a fog. I felt quite frightened of something unseen but horrifying. It made me realise how large and how varied the world was and how many different people lived in it in ways we did not know or see. Granny handed over lots of parcels with food and clothes no doubt; I think she made many visits there.

One Christmas, my parents went to New Zealand so on Christmas Day Granny gave me a huge brown paper parcel, labelled From Mummy and Daddy. As I undid the parcel, I saw just what I had wished for, a wicker dolls' pram, but then I wondered just how the postman could have carried such a parcel – was it really from my parents? When I questioned her, she made an acceptable diplomatic answer which made the deception bearable, but I never liked the dolls' pram as much as I should have. Granny always looked one in the eye and she had the bluest eyes I have ever seen, inherited by most of her children, grandchildren and even some great grandchildren. It is said you see a man's soul through his eyes. I believe this – those very blue eyes you see right through usually shine out from an honest good soul. They were such a great joy and excitement, those visits to Welton for Christmas with all the cousins, wonderful parties, Christmas trees and presents and spoiling but this had to end. So we were packed up and off we set on our return journey – piling onto the train, changing in Carlisle under the stationmaster's supervision, to be disgorged from the local train onto a tiny platform in what looked like miles of heather covered hills, and so back to Murrayton. Then the time came when my parents decided to move south where they could hunt, and be near my mother's family – so we moved. It was hard to say goodbye to the shepherds, but one wise one said, 'Jean, don't mind. Your home is where you make it,' and so it has been ever since.

Then it was decided that I should go to a convent school, St Mary's in Wantage, when I was about fourteen – what a very different world this was. I loved learning and meeting lots of the girls, but I soon began to feel I was being swept into something not so good, too. Of course the chapel, the choir which I was in, the readings and teachings were a major part, and who better to learn from than gentle, holy nuns – but the girls *en masse* were not always nice. I was told by one of their hierarchy that I had to be in love with one of the senior girls and be her lady-in-waiting (all secret), so to go along with this strange behaviour I chose a pretty girl and strung along for a while. I suddenly realised how alien and how idiotic this was to me, and what sheep people are – one person standing out against the crowd for good or bad can change it. I learnt to have the courage of my convictions early; not always easy. So to my contemporaries' horror, I confronted the senior girl, explaining that my declaration was not true and that I thought it all rubbish. The underworld of emotion was shaken, but as a result I found there were other rebels who needed only a catalyst to follow suit. One friend and I made secret expeditions over the wall to the funfair three days running, probably while the nuns were in chapel – we were also allowed off on bikes and my friend used to meet a boyfriend who was a jockey. I was paid off in chocolates to lie in wait with the bikes – her mother was a famous trainer and would have exploded with rage had she known.

One of the most important occasions at St Mary's was confirmation. We were prepared for this months before – it was a big build-up, but I was not particularly impressed until the chosen Sunday arrived for the bishop's visit and the service. We had been on a silent retreat for two days, which at fifteen was really hard. Not to be able to talk seemed incredible and the tension built up. Then came the service at which the wonderfully robed bishop performed – when he laid his hands on my head, I suddenly felt different – very relieved and somehow free of any cares. It was the feeling I have had since whenever I give and receive healing – a miraculous feeling of being filled with light. But as I looked down at the bishop's feet, I suddenly noticed that this saintly man had forgotten to remove his galoshes – it was so right to be able to laugh at a moment filled with joy. Of course we had a good lunch and festival celebrations, but though I felt different from then on of course through time I did not always recollect this feeling.

My faith really was founded by Sister Edith Cecil, my favourite nun, who was a milestone of great importance in my life. She was small and round, very plain, and wore thick, pebble glasses. She was a brilliant academic. I had a lot of coaching lessons on my own with her (as my previous schooling was nil), so we had much time. She taught me Christianity. More, she enabled me to have knowledge and faith. She talked about many theological subjects, which fascinated me, and she laid the seeds of my whole religious learning and questioning. I have often remembered her in times of trouble, and been so grateful for her teaching. She told me to study the earliest Christianity known and in my old age I have had time to do this.

My father, Basil Falkner, in his hunting clothes

Years later I spent a week with Professor Quispel learning about some of the Dead Sea Scrolls found at Nag Hammadi, bought by him for Jung and translated and edited. His teaching was not esoteric, but about the historical facts and findings. I have studied Gnosticism, and this led me on to so much more. I recognised such a light from the soul of Sister Edith Cecil which I have met only in rare people since. From then on, I pursued the esoteric meaning of teachings. After I left the convent school, and up to the beginning of the war, there was a year when to my absolute delight I was sent to Paris. I was sent to stay with a French family who were relations of some people my mother had been to when she was a girl. Highly respectable, hard working, very typically French. I remember my father took me and I arrived with what now would be an immense trunk and my canary in a cage. I hadn't been abroad to other people's homes before and we arrived and struggled up the spiral staircase, or my father and Monsieur did, with my luggage and the canary. There to my horror I found in their drawing room a family gathering and friends sitting around on little gold chairs in a very formal way, sipping a thimbleful of rather strong liqueur. I remember having one horrified look and bursting into tears and my father, who could not take any form of emotional scene, simply said he would be in Paris, he certainly didn't tell me where, and fled.

But this was the beginning of the most marvellous year. I went to dressmaking classes, I learnt to cut cloth with Molyneux's seamstresses. I really learnt to sew and make clothes. I was taken by a very intelligent Mademoiselle most afternoons to see pictures and galleries, not much music, but an enormous lot else. Indeed it gave me a very great feeling for Paris and the French, which I have always kept, and also a love of sightseeing and enjoying beautiful things. I was allowed a certain amount of freedom on Sundays, because my father had very great Russian friends who lived in the most delightful atmosphere. My father's Russian friend known as Mily (Nicholas Miloradovich), a very great philosopher and related to the Russian royal family, said one or two things to me which have stuck all my life. One of the things he said was: 'Jean, never forget life is a chain of small miracles.' How right he was, and to my delight, I still keep up the connection with his family.

Not so long ago, to my great joy I was invited to Regensberg in Germany to the marriage of Mily's grand-daughter to a German prince Croy, head of one of the Austrian empire's most important families. This wedding was like a fairytale from the past. Hundreds of guests had been invited (I was almost the only English person), first to a dinner the night before the wedding. We arrived at this beautiful castle which was octagonal – with drawbridge and wide moat – all lit with chandeliers and candle light shining through a mass of small windows. There, a hundred people were gathered for a magnificent dinner – all in full evening dress – with carefully thought out seating plans. Waited on by local men and women in uniform and white gloves, we enjoyed food beyond description – it was so beautiful, like the best picture from a chef's book. The highlight was a whole boar. It was an evening I shall never forget. My neighbours were charming and interesting – we all had love of the bride and bridegroom in common. After the speeches, we circulated through all the rooms of the octagon – taking in the pictures and furnishings on the way. The next day, everyone assembled in wedding clothes – many of them in long evening dress, much jewellery and beautiful furs. Then the bride and family and all her escorts in full bridal regalia walked out of the castle, over the drawbridge, down the village street and into the church. The ceremony was a Russian Catholic wedding with the symbolic three crowns, incense and candles. After the service, the bride and groom, family and guests, walked back through the village over the drawbridge into the castle where a vast buffet lunch awaited us. The reception went on for many hours and much interesting conversation took place and many threads and connections were made. Many of the German relations and friends my age had fought a horrific war on opposite sides. Many had lost arms or legs and, like us, lost relations and friends, and yet on this happy family occasion of a holy union we all enjoyed each other's company and there was much to enjoy together like music, rising in harmony above all worldly happenings.

Back to Paris before the war, where I was allowed to spend Sundays with simply charming distant French relations – quite different from the family I lived with. This one was a very old French Huguenot family in some way related to my grandmother. They were very distinguished and most kind, I remember feeling extremely bewildered by a consciousness of world affairs when politics first came into my life as the French are always discussing politics, it was inevitable this should happen. My relations are a fairly close group of Cazenoves, who were Protestants. There were two sons my age. One, Jacques, used to spend his weekends distributing political leaflets, apparently very controversial; I remember he was a Royalist. The other, Aymar, looked most glamorous in soldier's uniform – huge white plumes in his helmet when in full dress; he was at the military academy at St Cyr. Sometimes we went to the races, and sometimes to deliver mysterious political pamphlets. They had many friends and relations and I enjoyed their company. In the summer they would take me with them to their charming villa covered with very strongly scented roses, on the coast near Dieppe at Pourville.

I returned from France full of foreboding. I had the impression there was going to be a war, and the French hated us. I remember trying to make myself heard (children are never listened to, especially when they just 'feel'). How right my premonition proved to be only a year later – at the time, no-one would listen to me, though I kept saying: 'There is going to be a war.'

There have been one or two times in my life when I have had a glimpse of situations in which I might later find myself, though at the time they seemed so far removed as to be impossible. One of the first of these flashes happened when I was home from school and my mother took me to a concert in Leicester, which was really a considerable distance from where we lived, to hear Sir Malcolm Sargent conduct the Huddersfield choir in one of their wonderful choral works. This made a tremendous impression, not only with the music, but the whole thing was so marvellously held together by Sir Malcolm Sargent. In the middle of the concert, I looked far below to see the conductor, and what I saw was this small, attractive, dynamic figure. I just said to myself, I know I'm going to marry that man. Well, marriage is a manner of speaking and it was very extraordinary how many years later I spent several years in a very close friendship and companionship with Malcolm Sargent and got to know him very well indeed and so did my children. But at that time it was so absolutely unlikely and outside the context of my life as to be really extraordinary.

At home, in spite of this feeling of heavy foreboding, life went on. I was just grown up and loved parties. There were a few dances in London of friends who were being debs. It was not my scene, and though I enjoyed the parties and the people, they were so much less fun than those in the country – people seemed rather shallow and weedy in London!

My grandfather gave a dance for me in their home, Welton Place. I

My father Basil Falkner

remember my grandfather, Harry Garrard, sending the chauffeur over to give me a most exquisite brooch he had had made for me – two hearts entwined with a wing at each end in diamonds (one half) and rubies (the other half) with a note saying: 'This comes with love from me to you until you find someone who is as proud of you as I am to give my half to.' This and the brooch my husband gave me years later were always my most precious possessions, though the gift from my grandfather sadly was stolen some years ago with much else from my house in London. The brooch Richard gave me is a huge diamond star and when I asked him why he'd given me this present, he said, 'Because you always keep going.' And it has kept me going for a long time since – it is called my 'keep going' brooch.

I had been the previous spring to stay with a French family in Switzerland in Lausanne, the Duc and Duchess Ducazes. Their daughter had stayed to hunt and I went back to ski. In those days there were very few ski-lifts, but the hard work was always worth it. We often went up to Villars where later in life I was to live with my husband and children. The visit to the Ducazes was interesting as many deposed royalty lived around and were much entertained – butlers in white gloves, and long lunches and receptions. The Duc was a great chef and very interested in food. This visit certainly widened my mind and was most enjoyable.

When I returned home once more I found the atmosphere very tense, though life seemed normal. We would have lovely supper picnics and flirted with dashing officers from the nearby cavalry school at Weedon – the army only had horses then. One evening we were playing hide-and-seek after supper in the woods, when my father arrived with an urgent message – all officers return to barracks at once. The next day after church war was declared. The date was 3 September 1939.

CHAPTER TWO

World War II and Post-war Travel

War – nursing – Radcliffe – Sir Harold Gilles' burns unit – post-war travels – au pair girl – London – Richard

WHILE WAITING TO TRAIN AS A NURSE I joined up as a VAD (war time nurse) and for a short time went to look after children evacuated from London. Then I went to nurse in a Polish hospital in the most romantic castle, Cortachy, in Scotland where the remains of the shattered Polish cavalry regiments gathered to recover after horrific escapes from occupied Poland. These were their crack cavalry regiments who were decimated by the Russians. The Poles were a revelation and an enormous awakening to a new vision of life. This was a very impressionable time

Nursing in World War II

for me. I was naïve about life, emotionally vulnerable and torn with grief for people who had suffered unimaginable tragedy and horror. I learnt enough Polish to communicate and French was our common language. My father once said angrily to me at a time when later I was looking for a job after the war, 'When I think of all the money I spent on your education and all you can do at the end of it is dance and speak French.' Little did he realise what very valuable assets both these things were. French has been invaluable all my life – and enjoyable – it has enabled me to deal with many situations I otherwise would have missed!

The Poles were shattered people, with terrible stories of horror and suffering. My first sight of a man with deep weals across his back from burns made by red hot iron bars – and much more was horrifying. They were such wonderful people, who having suffered so long through their history had an amazing courage and resilience. Their singing and music making and dancing were unforgettable. They were by nature like beautiful symphonies in a minor key – slightly sad. When I finally went to Poland in 1995, I felt this sadness in their country.

By the time the Polish army had reached Scotland, it had been through traumatic and horrific experiences, and to actually see the marks of torture and raw beatings on young men's bodies is a profound experience. They also were the most lovely people and I wondered whether because of their history of suffering, immense sensitivity and compassion had formed in their national character. I'll never forget the Christmas spent with the Poles; like being in a fairy tale, beautiful, wonderful singing, exquisite songs, decorations artistic beyond anything I had seen before; all made from next to nothing – bits and pieces found here and there, greenery from the garden, quite beautiful! The singing began on Christmas Eve and continued un-broken until Christmas night. They were attended by a priest named Father Andrew Glazewski, who communicated to many people after his death. That Christmas, the Poles created a little world within a world, and I made many Polish friends. One or two of them remained friends until they died not so long ago, having settled in England and married. Once, I climbed out of a small window in the castle to go to a party – not realising there was a deeper jump than I thought. A few days later, the pain in my foot had grown worse, and the doctor said I had broken a bone. I had to tell a very white lie as to how I'd done it – falling over the end of a bed, I said! I spent many weeks in plaster having a good time as I was unable to work, so I sat about mostly in the garden and was entertained by Poles and others who were convalescent patients. I learnt a lot about them and their country.

One time a ball was given at Glamis Castle to which the Polish officers and nurses were bidden. They taught me to dance the mazurka and they waltzed like Prince Charmings. Glamis was a terrifyingly spooky place but the evening had been so glamorous that I managed to shake off the morose atmosphere that filled the downstairs passages, where there were no people or festivities. I was taken by a member of the family to an unused part of the building where, it was rumoured, a relation had been walled in alive!

On the way home, driven by a saintly Red Cross commandant who had sat up all night, we saw the whole sky ablaze with fantastic coloured lights. These were the Aurora Borealis – the northern lights of Celtic myth and tales. It was an awesome experience to see the sky filled with all the colours of the rainbow. The heavens were lit up. It gave me the same feeling that I have since had in various places where dolmens stood and in holy places – literally an unearthly experience, and the colours are like those which I see inside my head while healing. The lights could have been from the mysterious place Hyperbora, from whence we came. The Poles' nickname for me was (in Polish) 'Sunshine'. Curious that years later in quite another hospital I was also nicknamed Sunshine (Cockney English this time!). I particularly remember a blind boy when he returned to hospital months after he had left, without prompting and only by hearing my footsteps, shouting out, 'Hello Sunshine.' I'm very glad they felt that about me. Life nursing the Poles at the castle in Scotland was a very emotional time. Every day I read the names in *The Times* of more and more of my friends killed in action. I used to take letters from my boyfriend to read by the river walk in beautiful surroundings. Then they stopped too, when he was killed. There were many other flirtations, but life seemed to go by so quickly and my nursing was really where my heart was. Of course, I fell in love with a Pole. Such an enigma – handsome, aristocratic and silent. He had shocked his parents by not conforming to their wishes and had left home to design sets for the Polish Ballet in Warsaw instead. The only times we had together were in my few hours off when we used to go and have high tea in the local town – a very dull little local town, but our conversation – or his – was always so fulfilling and his imaginative dialogue was an opening of my mind to things I had never heard about. At the end of the war, he found me again and I would have married him as he wished, but I was not brave enough to undertake what was then a seemingly huge plunge into the unknown – my social English life, family and friends also called – and won.

Very soon, I went to do my nursing training at the Radcliffe Infirmary at Oxford. One day while I was working as a junior probationer, into the ward came Professor Fleming. He was a most charming person and a very humble person with a great understanding of people. He took the trouble to explain to the junior probationers why our unattractive and rather menial tasks were terribly important and were a contribution to his new and explosive research work on penicillin. One patient died and one lived, which was due to penicillin. Very much later in the war, I administered penicillin to save the lives of hundreds of burnt patients, and then even later penicillin in synthetic form. But they were fairly grim years at the Radcliffe, in the first place because I was not very amenable to discipline, and secondly, lots of my contemporaries and boyfriends were in the army nearby and I couldn't understand at the age of seventeen why one should be expected to have such responsibility for lives on night duty, and yet be locked in at ten o'clock at night, and never allowed to have the occasional party or evening out. However, matron and I didn't really see eye to eye over this, and I left the Radcliffe and moved on. Much later towards the end of the war, while nursing in Sir Harold Gilles' plastic unit, I found myself getting to know Professor Fleming very well, and sharing sandwiches with him at lunchtime. He never changed, being a typical, rather shy Scotsman and a very humane person. It certainly was a great privilege to have known him and to have seen his work from early days and to have been part even in the smallest way in the history of penicillin.

During 1940, in November while I was at home on leave for twenty-four hours on our farm in Northants, Coventry was bombed. During the night, there were horrendous noises worse than any thunderstorm, and the whole sky lit up. It went on and on, then the noise of bombers thrumming through the sky was heard – it was the night of a very bright full moon. My father, who had been a POW in the 1914–18 war and had suffered ever since, came outside with me and he said, 'My God, they have got Coventry.' Indeed, the German bombers had got and flattened Coventry, but one bomber on his way home had offloaded his bomb on our farm. It blew out a whole huge field – next day there was just a crater. The sky had been ablaze and the crackling and smoke and aftermath was to be felt and a terrible sensation, a premonition took hold – I had already seen the fires and all those people in the ruins, wounded or dead – yet showing such inner light. Their courage subsequently was to become a landmark – an example to suffering people. This was the only time I ever saw my father cry. He was a very controlled, remote, shut up person, but this experience, so long after his own awful experiences, proved too much for him and he wept.

Years later after the war I went to the opening concert in the repaired Coventry Cathedral – repaired with the help of young Germans as well as English. The concert was the Berlin Philharmonic Orchestra conducted by the great Furtwängler – it was so very moving I felt I would explode. Coventry, the example of reconciliation.

Having left the Radcliffe, I took a job for a few months in an American hospital – a civilian Red Cross unit, set up, built and highly equipped and modern on the outskirts of Oxford. There was a plastic surgeon who employed me to help nurse patients who needed plastic surgery, and it was through him that I found my way to the most fulfilling job I ever had – a job nursing in the burns unit at Park Prewitt in Basingstoke for Sir Harold Gilles, the famous plastic surgeon. When I left Oxford for Basingstoke, some very kind friends had me to stay so I could work at the hospital daily. My friend Gill's father, Lord Perth, had been a well-known ambassador in Italy and was also first Secretary General of the League of Nations. I remember rather vaguely that he used to go on about treatment of the Jews, but the terrible truth is that it meant nothing to me nor my friends – how dreadful that people were so uninformed about the death camps. At that time, there was no mass communication like the media nowadays, of course, and we were very involved where we were with the wounded in hospital, but we should have been aware.

Rations were very short but my kind hosts had some of the American army to stay sometimes. They were an horrific invasion of new ways – new behaviour, new language, and with quite a different approach to life. Rationing for them did not exist, and they had all their own supplies. But one day as I was leaving early for hospital, I looked into the dining room and there I saw the American visitor polishing off Lord Perth's last few tots of his previous weekly whisky ration – too awful to behold; another time this same unfortunate visitor finished up Lord Perth's remaining marmalade ration. It stood before him in a pot and he just poured it over his bacon. We all had a lot to learn but Lord Perth's beautiful manners and his control was exemplary – he merely gasped. Rationed food was just adequate but certainly very precious and at times I was hungry. Noticeably though, everyone was much healthier and this has now been proved – we have not benefited from surplus food in this country.

Sir Harold Gilles was indeed a great man, artistic, a brilliant plastic surgeon, with a great love of people and life with compassion and an understanding of people. He had a wonderful sense of humour. I nursed in the operating theatre and also in the burns unit and here, in spite of the sadness, there was enormous gladness too. It was so wonderful to see people who had come in so terribly disfigured, who after some years really would be able to be normal looking enough to face the world and their families. It was here that many realisations about life came to me. One very great awakening that I had was how really unimportant people's physique was, and I began to understand how to see the essence of people, the reality behind the mask. After seeing a whole row of soldiers carried in on stretchers, labels on some part of their anatomy bearing name or number, without faces, some with just holes, I came to know and to recognise them later if they survived, as people, each absolutely unique, each a complete individual. These were people with such humour, such courage and who were such an example. How much I learnt from them of endurance and keeping going. There was a lovely incident one night when I was on night duty with another nurse, and a huge convoy of burned people were coming in. We were alerted in the operating theatre that Sir Harold Gilles was driving down from London to operate, everything was got ready in a great flurry in a tense atmosphere, instruments laid out, patients wrapped in green operating towels, lights ablaze, theatre nurses scrubbed up – when with a roar the great man himself appeared at the door of the operating theatre in long white cotton underpants and vest. I had prepared every last thing except his operating gown. He did laugh which was the greatness of him; laughter dissolves tension and all was restored and the operations went ahead.

I think, although I was not conscious of it at this time, that healing hands must have inevitably helped people. I remember always being the nurse who was asked, frequently pleaded with, to go down to the operating theatre and hold the hand of whoever was about to have some horrific operation. This certainly was not because I had blue eyes because many of them could not even see or were swathed in bandages and certainly had no view of me so there must have been something else that they felt, some empathy that they felt was comforting, consoling. I think almost all nurses have healing hands because what is it that makes somebody want to be a nurse in the first place? But I suppose some dare show it or dare do what they feel like doing more than others. I think at a very early age we become conditioned and self-conscious, where it would be better if we were more like children and more spontaneous.

Years later, when I did meals on wheels in London, I found that in the ten minutes I was allowed to spend with people, touching a shoulder, holding a hand or putting an arm around the shoulders, was really of more value to the people than was the food, because these lonely people needed feeding on a spiritual as well as a human level – they often just would stand and want their hands held or an arm put round them just to know there was another human being with whom they were in real contact, and who minded about them and showed compassion. Another lesson in life of learning the value of people took place in the burns unit of the hospital. One grim day I walked into the ward and there were rows of stretchers (just after D-day when men had died in thousands landing on the enemy beaches) of wounded men lying on the ground, each with a label with name, number etc. One particular body had no face, only eyes and a hole with four teeth where the mouth and jaw should have been – and yet as I passed, I heard a loud wolf whistle – made by this wreck. This nearly broke my spirit, my emotions overcame me and having managed some kind of reply, I fled to cry. The courage and humour of those men was an example we should not only never forget, but strive to learn, teach and emulate. People no longer seem to be made of the same calibre – whinging was unknown. One smile, one look, one word, one wolf whistle at the right time can not only change someone's life but also their whole outlook on life and can give a lesson in wholeness. My feet were kept on the ground too – oh, the awful stench of bandages from burned bodies that had to be washed by hand and re-rolled. The sickening smell that got into one's very skin, eyes, nose, hair. I remember it still. I smelt it again even during the film *The English Patient.* Oh, the courage of men in pain that I saw. How dare any of us complain, ever.

I was sad that I just didn't manage to nurse up until the end of the war. I punctured my rubber glove in the operating theatre and picked up some new streptococci virus which had grown resistant to penicillin and which created havoc in my body, particularly under all my fingernails. I won't go into details of the awful pain and illness I suffered for a while at this period and I was also in a very depressed and shattered state. In fact I was invalided out just before the end of the war.

It is extraordinary the way people who do healing, who are healers, emenate a kind of energy and aura that will attract others who are open to this. People who have compassion, people who are also healers, also attract people who need healing, like a kind of magnet.

I have observed that on another level people who wear a certain uniform also having a presence themselves, emenate this energy which is aided by virtue of their uniform. In fact a nurse in uniform, a priest in priest's clothes, a policeman, all give out an air of authority. They give people a feeling usually of security without ever having to communicate at all. It was interesting that a policeman told me once that he was walking down a very crowded King's Road in plain clothes and he got bashed about and jostled as we all do. The next time he walked down the busy street he was in his uniform and he had a space of about eighteen inches all about him. I have often found in a gathering, not all of healers but of mixed kinds of people, in a room filled with hundreds of people, one will catch the one eye and that eye will come to you and will either ask a question that needs a real answer or will make some observation, or a statement, that enables one to link in on another and much deeper level of understanding.

When I recovered and the war was over also in the east, I spent a year of almost total abandonment. War was over but life suddenly had to change. I was very ill, not only with poisoned fingers, but from shattered nerves. I had wonderful, good friends, Mike and Elizabeth Lyle who lived in Scotland, who had me to stay for some months. Michael had during my nursing years come into the hospital wounded, which was a coincidence – I had to be excused from that particular operation – it would be too hard to see a friend on the operating table – and he recovered but was invalided out. They lived up in the hills in a very remote part of Perthshire, and it was here with them that I recovered and put myself together again. Elizabeth's father was an important Minister of Air. He arrived to stay with an infection which involved three-hourly penicillin injections – what to do? The doctor unable to visit all those times entrusted me. So for three days and nights I gave him what then were very painful and crude penicillin injections. He was very polite and formal and I remember laughing even in those circumstances when at 2 a.m. he would say, 'Thank you very much, Miss Falkner,' (no Christian name terms even). He made a good recovery. I stayed on enjoying a wonderful family life in this beautiful, remote place until I had regained control; then I had to return home and find a job.

This was a time of complete irresponsibility and fun which I have hardly ever known again until now, but to work I went to Switzerland to be an au pair to a very well-known Swiss doctor's two small boys. Dr Ducrey had a clinic in the Swiss mountains in Montana. It was a clinic where important, powerful and political people from all over Europe stayed. They were taking refuge, political or otherwise, as well as cures. There were also many sick people suffering from the aftermath of the war. Many had been in the death camps and had been prisoners in the holocaust and had just survived.

The great adventure of getting out of England was a revelation. The sense of freedom and independence was glorious and I began to realise that we were an insular people – being on the Continent felt somehow more like belonging, not only to England but to the universe.

On the way to my job, I was to pay a visit to good friends who were at the Belgian Embassy in Berne. I took a boat, then a train. The thrill of going to sleep in a couchette and waking up at the frontier was unimaginable. I had travelled before, but during the war years I had forgotten the excitement, and also the slight fear. I remember at one stop during the night when I got off the train to buy a cup of coffee being offered on the platform, I saw to my horror the train slowly moving on – no way of getting on. I was so shocked I think I just I just stood still. Then I saw that mercifully the train was only being shunted into another bay. I was relieved to get back into my carriage. I duly arrived at the embassy where not only was I with my friends, but in unimaginable luxury – and the bliss of eating white bread with cherry jam un-rationed seemed hardly real.

It was only now I really realised how we had been quite short of food in the war. Not only was it rationed (an adequate amount), but it was dull and of bad quality. I remember hospital meals as one long dreary succession of dried fish and boiled cabbage, potatoes and beetroot. The worst deprivation was of sweet things – and to this day I appreciate chocolate as a great treat. It was a very rare commodity then. The most agonising temptation nursing in hospital was when having to clear out soldiers' lockers, in which chocolate (the most precious present then) brought by loving relations was stacked up because the soldier probably had no jaw nor mouth, having stepped on a landmine. So chocolate was there, but only to look at.

Staying at the embassy, I met a very good-looking, young Belgian; dark curly hair, blue eyes and a devastating smile. I was astonished to hear he was a Dominican monk, known as Dodo, and that he was also going to stay with the doctor's family where I was going to work. So after a few enjoyable days in a free world, we proceeded together to Lausanne. There, we were to stay with the family in a hotel for a few weeks before going to the mountains. Madame Doctor was typically Swiss, short, tough, humourless and rather too careful with money. There were two small boys, one fat and slow, called Peachli (peach!), the other small, quick and very naughty. I had to take them to various classes and for walks and not too much else until later to ski. In my spare time I went to visit a very beloved Swiss girl called Marthe who had been in Scotland as our au pair. She was an enchanting, gay person, by this time happily married and the patronne of her husband's cake shop. To have tea with our dear Marthe in her cake shop was like heaven.

Being pretty naïve, I did not notice until after a while the flirtation between Madame and Dodo – but when I thought about it, my mind boggled – how could a priest be staying in such close proximity to a lady? Strange, though, that many years later, Dodo left the priesthood. He was the first person since the nun at school taught me about Christianity with whom I felt I could talk about my faith. I remember a conversation about the power of prayer during which he so clearly believed in the power of prayer that I had no further doubts myself. His words have stuck with me ever since. Prayer generates a certain powerful holy energy – felt in churches and convents and indeed wherever groups of people pray together, and in hermit's cells where there is constant prayer. This holy energy is also in many holy places which can be hundreds of years old and in ruins. One such place is the abbey at Glastonbury – sitting in the ruins early one morning with closed eyes, I felt the place was full of white-robed monks praying – the feeling was so strong that I forgot where I was.

Once I was travelling in Ireland on the west coast, a rocky, strange place called the Burren, and I came across ruined and beautiful Corcomroe Abbey – there the holy feeling was strong. On Iona, a very holy island, there are many places where this energy can be felt. One such place I sat in, a stone circle, was reputed to be where St Columba meditated on first landing on Iona. He must most surely have felt the energy places in which to pray and on which to build.

In France, most pilgrim gathering places and hundreds of shrines have this same feeling. To feel the energy of Chartres Cathedral is another awesome experience. It fact it was so overwhelming in the cathedral that I had to go and sit outside and ground myself before going on round; it's also strong in Vézelay, the gathering place of pilgrims at the third crusade, with its cathedral built to light high on a hill, from where I later went on a pilgrimage myself. It is there again in the cell of the hermitage outside Assisi in which St Francis prayed – with one window and a view you see in holy pictures – the same view that was painted by Giotto and adornes the Basilica in Assisi. The same energy and view was in the chapel in the south west of Scotland, where St Ninian gazed out on the Scottish sea and blue hills when he built the first church and taught Christianity ... and so many others – but in all these places people have prayed through the years and perpetuated the holy energy. To gaze into the distance is to gaze into infinity.

Working in Montana with the Ducreys was most illuminating. The conversation at meals, since special people were always invited to the doctor's house, was tremendously informative and interesting. I think it was here that I probably learnt more about the war than I had during it, because I had been so involved in my own nursing tasks that I seemed to have been rather unconscious of what was going on in the rest of the world.

But at this stage, to meet Italians and Germans who were political refugees and hear them talk was fascinating and very revealing. Of course to my total horror there were also one or two people who were survivors of Auschwitz and Dachau and this really left an impression. I became conscious of what terrible things man does to man. They were not at all how I would have expected them to be, not the triumphant survivors, nor the conquering heroes. They were terribly bitter and completely disorientated and terribly sad. Of course, this was the very early stages and most of them, or certainly the one or two with whom I kept in contact for a while, reorientated themselves and have since made a life. But again at this time, before the terrifying facts of the death camps were known publicly, one could hardly believe them.

It was here that I met the famous pianist Dinu Lipparti and got to know him as I tried to teach him English. He was with his mistress and lover, the Romanian Princess Cantacuzino who had been his patron in Romania. He had been commissioned to play at a concert in her palace at a musical evening. They fell in love and she left her prince and eloped with Dinu to Europe. They were caught at the outbreak of war in Switzerland. Dinu sadly had TB and was ill. To hear him play was literally a heavenly experience – especially his interpretation of Chopin. I met him and the princess in later years when he came with her to London to play at a concert but he was dying. What a great loss!

Life was very varied and I think typical of lots of young people's lives after the war. Lots of friends in the army in Germany came to visit while on leave, and we had some wild parties – a time of carefree living. People who came from England on holiday were only able to spend the meagre amount of money allowed out of England. I also had army friends who were in the clinic – ways had to be devised of getting them out in the evenings to parties. My problem was how to climb back into the Ducreys' chalet afterwards without the stairs creaking – quite a feat. This was a time for reflection, with great necessity for moments of stillness. These became more important to me in spite of the good life. I was not a great success as an au pair. I refused to take Madame's dull daughter dancing with me and in a rage she sacked me. When my money ran out, I went and lived with a family whose head man was the village carter. I slept in their living room, and shared the food they ate, with one bowl, and one spoon. It was the most delicious food, like muesli and yoghurt and black cherries which had been bottled in the summer. Simple and good.

I then went on to visit Italian relations and this was another marvellous experience. I learned to appreciate beautiful things and was bitten by the sightseeing bug which has remained with me for the rest of my life, because my Italian cousins were immensely proud, which all Italians are, of their country. I stayed with them in their country house Fraforiano near Venice, and also in Rome. They did take a lot of trouble, although they were young men of my own age, to show me all the beautiful things there were, and being shown beautiful things by those to whom they belong is far the best way to get an impression and to enjoy them.

Returning to London, I set up a kindergarten in my Chelsea flat. After the war many of my friends were married with children, and begged my help, so I felt it would be a good idea to start a kindergarten. I did six months as a training teacher at a small private school and became very interested in the Montessori teaching method. I realised the thrill of giving children something, enabling them to learn reading and writing and hearing it come back almost like an echo with their version of what you had taught. This was the most marvellous and satisfying time. It was much easier in fact to teach other people's children, with whom I was not emotionally involved, than it ever was later on to teach and help my own.

This was a very good time; my small kindergarten flourished, I taught children in the morning and I had marvellous opportunities in the holidays to travel. I had lots of different experiences and it is interesting in retrospect to observe that every single one of my travels has been for some reason. It now seems each one was an experience which I had to go through to understand people who later came to me for help. People who had the same situations, difficulties maybe, and so on. We were able to share experiences and sometimes release tensions.

On one of my trips to Switzerland, I joined up one evening with some older friends, Elizabeth and Rollo Hoare, to make up a foursome at one of those amusing Swiss evenings in the local eating, dancing bistro. They had been joined by another man, a good friend of theirs, whom I wasn't particularly interested in. He was a very tall, silent man and

My husband,
Richard Meade-Fetherstonhaugh

the most off-putting thing was that he had a large black moustache. I've never cared for men with either moustaches or beards, so that was the end of that, I thought. He was to be my future husband, Richard.

Our wedding, August 1948

CHAPTER THREE

Marriage and Uppark

**Richard – marriage – Uppark – Sarah's appearance –
honeymoon travels – Uppark – Annie – Stella – Wales –
Harriet – deerkeepers – Emma – Bransbury – Sophie –
travels – Spain – Calella**

ONE YEAR LATER, in London, the younger sister of this couple I had
dined with in Switzerland rang me in desperation. She said: 'Please,
please come, I need one girl more to make up a dinner party. My
brother-in-law and sister are still skiing and they have landed me with a
huge dinner party for a charity dance!'

At that time, I was suffering from one of my many setbacks, after what
I thought had been a passionate love affair. Later, I realised that there
was only ever one real love in my life, but at that time it had been a
rebuff and I was in a very depressed state and nearly didn't go to the
dinner; then a kind of energy pushed me into decision that I felt incapable
of resisting.

When I arrived, there were about twelve people. I found myself sitting
next to that same tall, silent man, but without the moustache. I thought
he looked very nice. He didn't talk very much and if he did I can't
remember at all what about. On my right was a very attractive, old friend
of my family whom I hadn't seen for years, and he and I talked pretty
much constantly throughout dinner. When we reached the party, the tall,
silent man asked me to dance. He only performed fairly well but he asked
me to dance again and that was that. Well, two days after the party I
had a letter, and I had to think very hard who it was from; someone
called Richard asked would I meet him for tea at the Ritz. Of course
after a few months it turned into dinner and evenings out. Then we often
stayed for weekend parties in country houses, which was tremendous fun
with friends we had in common, and it was obvious that we clicked.
When Richard did propose marriage to me I was so overwhelmed at the
real thing and the awesome idea of actually being married that I simply

was unable to answer. In fact I took about three weeks really examining myself on a very deep level to make quite sure I could undertake what I felt was the most enormous commitment. Again, I felt pushed by this extraordinary energy coming from without, and with such a force that it overcame reasoning. I have since learned to respect this instinct and act on it. But still, little did I know of the enormousness of this task and the shape or form it would take, but at the time it certainly seemed a big step. I wish many young people who marry hastily today would ponder very much longer on the meaning of a marriage. It isn't just a wonderful, prolonged love affair where everyone lives happily ever after. It is a marriage of souls, and souls need to be married to be able to communicate on a very deep level. Richard was really a very mysterious person, he lived in a kind of world which seemed to be removed from this everyday world. I realise now that he was in fact a very advanced soul, almost a mystic. It must have been very hard for him to be earthed and weighed down by me because I was intensely domesticated and practical when we first got married and busy with having babies and so on. What a lot marriage opened up to me, and what an awakening and what an awareness began then. I know now that it was preparation for what lay ahead.

Richard had not told me anything about his home, only his deeper and inner thoughts and feelings, but a friend said to me, 'Oh, he lives in one of the most beautiful houses in England.' I thought to myself, 'Good. I shall enjoy arranging it'. Little did I know just what the word arranging would turn into. I arrived to stay at Uppark in West Sussex one Friday evening, and I was greeted effusively by two elderly people, my future parents-in-law, and shown into a small sitting-room of this large house. I could not see at first, but through the darkness I made out their shapes crouched over a one-bar electric fire, in terrible cold. I was given a small supper on a tray as dinner at eight was long over, and shown up to bed. I had during my journey developed a dreadful cold, I am sure from fear, so I felt rather strange, but stranger still in this large, hideously furnished room. Exhausted, I slept. During the night I suddenly woke up. The door opened and a lady came in and bent over me – she was beautiful, she was very serious and she had on a rustling, taffeta dress. I then noticed a man behind her, with long curly hair. The surprise and the shock, I suppose, woke me up. Then I realised that it was dark. I put the light on and there was no-one there. When people from another dimension appear, it is neither light nor dark, and it is timeless. I didn't feel unduly surprised, I simply accepted it, turned over and went to sleep. The next

Uppark

Emma, Harriet, Sophie and Tiggy on Harriet's knee

day my father-in-law was showing me round the house and as we walked into the red drawing room, we turned around and he pointed to a portrait over the door, telling me this was the first Lady Fetherstonhaugh, Sarah. I looked, and there she was, the lady I had seen in the night, who had come to have a look at me. I nearly fainted from surprise, it was awesome. Sarah did have a good look at me and then faded away for many years. She appeared through the years and was around in essence but I never saw her again as clearly. She appeared and was very much around years later, when the house burned down, and again when it was being rebuilt and when we moved back in.

Sarah must have been a beautiful person. I thought very much about her, her presence and her exquisite taste. This enabled her and Sir Matthew to redecorate their house not only with taste but with money. Her family were French Huguenot bankers and we know Sir Matthew inherited a fortune. I found trunks in the attic into which she had put examples of earliest chintz and materials presumably not selected along with wallpapers – some of which can be seen in the Victoria and Albert Museum.

Sir Matthew seems to have been a rather serious person. He devised a method of shorthand. He kept meticulous accounts of all the things he bought. Sarah painted many charming small pictures of flowers, birds, butterflies and insects copied from some of their books; Edward's bird books and many volumes of Buffon. These pictures were quite out of proportion and some included most unlikely combinations of insects but they are obviously hers and she must have spent a lot of time doing them. Perhaps they were both too serious. Did they spoil their precious and most attractive son Harry – or did they not give him enough attention?

He was obviously a very gregarious person – filled the house with people. He loved hunting and in one of Fernley's books there is a reference to him hunting with the Meynell Hunt. His own hunt ran over many miles, as far as Rogate.

Harry's early portrait depicts a most attractive but rather weak looking person. At a very early age he saw Emma Hamilton doing her poses in a London nightclub, and the story is well known of how he took her to live with him at Uppark. She is reputed to have danced on the dining room table for gentleman after dinner. She must have been very bored at Uppark while Sir Harry hunted and raced – no-one would have entertained her and she found solace in the village. After one of his prolonged trips away, Sir Harry returned to find her pregnant and turned her out. Evidently, though, at some point during her stay at Uppark she had met Greville who had suggested to her that if she needed help to turn to him. This she did, and was taken in by Greville and shipped to Naples to be housekeeper to his uncle, Sir William Hamilton. It was here that she met Nelson, and the ensuing love story is famous. The ménage-à-trois seemed to have worked happily until Nelson died. It seems Emma was adrift, took to drink, was penniless and there was a sad little letter from her to Sir Harry asking for money. This he evidently sent her and he kept her IOU. He must have had a soft spot for her, even in his very old age. It is said that when Sir Harry turned Emma out, he also destroyed all evidence of her sojourn there, but there was one print left on the wall of the famous print room that included a picture of Emma.

I didn't tell my parents-in-law about Sarah's appearance, nor did I ask if she had appeared before because they were Victorian in outlook, conventional and difficult to communicate with. I felt they would not have understood.

Talking with my father-in-law, a very distinguished admiral, I asked him what I should call him. Admiral seemed too formal, Jim too informal, so what was it to be? He said he could not think of a solution. So I said I would have to call him 'I Say' until he did. Next day I had a charming note saying, 'Dear DIL what a fine idea,' signed, 'I Say', which he was called ever after that, DIL (daughter-in-law) being his riposte.

I was amazed by the house – it was so beautiful, full of light and sun and the beauty of the white and gold saloon was impressive, but the house had strange and very powerful vibrations which were seductive and destructive, proved by events later.

Uppark was built on a very old site where there had probably been a farmhouse – it was too high for water but there were huge dew ponds, chalk-bottomed big basins. In the present house the basement rooms, well underground, have arched, stone ceilings which certainly were there before the house was built in 1696. It lay on very powerful energy lines, and as a dowser I have felt these. The light power and the dark power are very strong at Uppark. One day I climbed to the top of the highest Down on the estate. It used to be a place where beacons were lit, and they say that at the time of the Armada this was a signalling site. I felt very peculiar and sat down, I seemed to be out of time and horrid things were happening – there was a huge fire and I knew there were blood sacrifices going on. Down below in the valleys, dark with juniper trees, are covered ways where Druids drove their cattle. Many prehistoric artefacts have been found on these sites; I went to see some at the British Museum – a pair of gold hair rings, apparently. Handling them gave me the same feeling I had felt sitting on the top of the Downs. They were not hair rings but had probably been worn around the ears, I felt. Saxon jewellery had also been found. One summer, archaeologists dug nearby and found many graves with whole skeletons in them. There had been an encampment here of alien peoples who were very large, unlike the then indigenous people who were short. I was impressed by their unimpaired teeth, and my dentist told me this was because they ate whole, uncooked grains.

Once, in my dreaming time at Uppark, I saw a whole crowd or tribe of little people streaming up the valley and up between the hills in the park to a place on top. I dowsed for energy/ley lines and found they had followed this exact route.

Richard and I were married in London, and had a wonderful wedding in St Luke's Church, Chelsea. Hundreds of friends came and a magnificent reception was held at a house in Cheyne Walk. It was still at a time of rationing but I don't remember there being restrictions on food and drink that day. I did, though, have to have my wedding dress made of curtain material, as clothes were still rationed. We were married by Richard's friend Barney Lawrence, who had been a prisoner of war with him, and priest to the people of the remote island of Tristan da Cunha. He had no experience of weddings, he said, but he made it very special even so; a great friend and a good man.

We went off on honeymoon and a grand tour – Richard was rather proud of his large car, an Armstrong Siddeley with a very long bonnet which later proved tricky to turn in tight spots. Driving to our destination, a friend's castle in Austria, we had to go over some mountains and I was to be the map reader. In those days I don't remember the roads having different categories, and I checked the route from A to B on what appeared to be a straight road. As we drove, the road began to climb – and climb rapidly until it became steep and then so steep I was holding on to the side with a vice-like grip to keep upright, but Richard just drove. He admitted later that he felt there was nothing else to do. We eventually reached the top of a very high mountain pass where small rocks were falling down beside us and could not be heard landing below. So down the other side we had to go – Richard had put on both the brake and bottom gear, but we slid and were ricocheting from one bend to the next. Eventually we landed on the straight. On arrival, our host told us that we had come over a pass that the army had deemed unfit for jeeps in the war. We had come the wrong way, but we'd arrived.

One night our host took us to a party. This was the tale ... it was like a fairy tale.

We set off to drive up a very steep mountain road with hairpin bends; on many of the bends, a farmworker was standing dressed in chainmail, as they would have been in the middle ages, holding burning brands. When we arrived at the top, at a huge square castle, we were shown into a courtyard in the middle of which was an assembled throng of Austrians all dressed in their colourful national dress; the girls in dirndls, and the men in lederhosen. There was a huge accordion band that played all evening and long tables laden with food and drink. Our host, Prince Khevenhuller, was an impressive figure and over his shoulders he wore a long black cloak until the dancing began. It went on all night; by the time we went home, the burning brands had long become ashes, and the dawn was streaking the sky.

Another day, we were taken to lunch with a local landowner who had a family of twelve sons. We sat down to lunch, and, sitting next to him, he told me how, during the war, he had been head of the Austrian Red Cross. 'But,' he said, 'my son sitting over there was a Nazi, so he turned me in, so I spent most of the war interned.' I was flabbergasted; there they were, only two years after the war, happy and together again. There was much of this treachery and fraternising in Austria and other Continental countries, but we who live on an island can have no idea what it is like to live in an occupied country. Our host went on to tell me that two of his gamekeepers were shot without warning in the woods by the Russian guards, because it was on the border. These people were still suffering like so many others, caught up in the aftermath of the war, which though peace had been signed was in a way still going on.

Some days later, driving in the Italian Alps, an almost worse driving episode occurred. We knew the name of our small village destination, but not the way. Following what looked like a possible route, we motored miles into bleak mountainous country, climbing at the same time. After what seemed like hours, by then going very slowly as the road got rougher and rougher, I joked that it looked as if we would end up with the wheels over the sides of the road – many a true word spoken in jest. It became grim, then seeing two peasants working in the rocks high up, we shouted: 'Please, which way?' In local Italian dialect which neither of us understood, the gist of it seemed to be, 'On, on, two or three days.' We understood better when after another few hundred yards the road narrowed and turned into a footpath fit only for donkeys and men – it was two to three days walk! We had to make a terrifying manoeuvre to turn back. We were by then quite exhausted and in was dark. We must have arrived eventually but I don't remember how! But these drives and many more with Richard, who seemed undisturbed, taught me how to do the same. I was never apprehensive, even driving alone across France to Spain with three small children. It was a good lesson in confidence.

Back from honeymoon to Uppark, I began to realise its energies – so many people came and went and I've seen how when they arrived at Uppark, as charming, nice and mostly quite ordinary people, some suddenly turned into really unpleasant, egotistical, power-ridden and even quite destructive people. It seems that Uppark tests people out. Many have had the worst brought out in them. The good ones have become much stronger in their goodness; they have improved and become wiser.

My parents-in-law were hard people to live with, but this is what I took on with marriage. Soon after we were married, Richard gave me a choice – should we go and live in South Africa where he was well, had great interest and had invested his money? We would have been very well off and Richard probably would have had good health because it was dry there and he was asthmatic, or should we live at Uppark, putting all we had into a bottomless well, which such old houses are?

The park was poor farmland, and would never pay for its upkeep. It had been a deer park and deer kept returning to eat crops and trees. The village cottages were almost derelict and endlessly needed, like the house, huge repairs and upkeep. What made me choose Uppark? I knew that Richard loved the place very dearly, and I knew that this was really what he wanted, in spite of the hardship. Again, this energy outside of me and reason took over and almost compelled me to choose Uppark. Families and family life are history. Richard, I knew, really wanted to keep the continuity going, and he did realise the struggle it would be, but we chose to make our lives at Uppark, weaving into the tapestry our own threads.

Years later, in 1954, we were offered the choice of struggling on or giving the house to the National Trust. An anonymous benefactor bequeathed the money to make this possible. This body at that time made gentlemen's agreements, pleasant to all concerned, and the people in the National Trust were dear friends and who very well understood the way of life in the kind of house Uppark is. They were charming, cultured, not too professional people, many of whom became great friends.

But, as we shall see, this turned out to be a great error. We trusted a trust, and Uppark was given on condition, quite absolutely, unquestionably, that the family should always live there. No home is a home without its history and the family who have lived in it and loved it all their lives and by previous generations, adding, subtracting, but keeping it in the family. The house had a soul with the essence of all the various people who had each contributed the best of their lives to it. People had given their time, love, energy and money, all to making it beautiful and keeping it that way. The eventual outcome for the house was a tragedy.

When I arrived at Uppark as a bride, I was taken round and introduced to various people who lived in the Uppark cottages and who had or still do work on the estate. There was an especially dear couple whose family had always lived in one of the thatched cottages at the bottom of the hill. In fact their family had lived there since the early eighteenth century, and their names were in the old wages book.

The old man spoke in such a broad Sussex dialect that I had difficulty understanding him, but he used to tell me of the days when wearing his smock, he'd walk up the hill to the stables where before work they were all given a loaf of bread, a hunk of venison and a pint of beer brewed in the brew house there. His job was to feed the deer with the best hay and to see to the deer fences, beautifully made iron railings which kept them in. His elderly wife would curtsey when she said, 'How d'you do, Ma'am,' and she wore her hair in a little tight bun skewered through with a real old-fashioned pin at the back of her head.

Their granddaughter, Annie, came to work for me when we lived in the park at Deerkeepers, and they have been loyal friends to this day. Annie once told me how her aunt worked in the house, and that her job had been to scrub the underground passages. She did nothing else throughout her life in service and she never went upstairs. Another very old lady visited the house one day and said her mother used to work there as under housemaid and had also never been upstairs. One day, her superior fell ill and told her to go and Brasso the brass stair-rod up the front stairs. She was so nervous that she did her job but she didn't dare look up so she never saw the ceilings nor the upstairs of the house. Another story was told by a man who was so ancient that nobody actually knew how old he was – he was called Pook and only had one tooth left in his head. He always walked up the hill to work for me in the garden, as he didn't trust cars and things, he said. When he was a lad he used to go with the baker's cart to deliver bread and fish and parcels. One day, on returning to the village, he discovered he'd forgotten to leave the fish at the big house and was told to go back, but by then it was dark. He started off up the hill but arrived at a haunted spot and ran off with fright, chucking the parcel in the pond. He said he thought no-one had ever noticed.

One person from the village was to come in and out of my life. I first met Stella when she came up to the big house to see my mother-in-law, Lady Meade-Fetherstonhaugh, with another girl to be interviewed about working for me and my mother-in-law. Annie was delegated to me – I was living at Deerkeepers in the park – and Stella was to work in the big house under a very fierce, highly professional housekeeper. Stella learned a great deal from the housekeeper. She was the best housekeeper herself I have ever known. She knew exactly how to clean everything, the eighteenth-century steel firearms, all the brass in its different forms, silver things, gilt things, glass, china, furniture, everything. Stella worked all her life at Uppark and in the village in Harting. She lived in an old Uppark cottage which her family had lived in for generations. She worked in the big house until my MIL left and then she worked for me in quite a different way just for a morning a week, and then when I moved to the walled garden cottage she worked for me there. She followed me wherever I lived, and when my three daughters grew up and married she went round and worked for them all for one morning a week. On and on through the years, when the grandchildren arrived, she was part of their lives. Stella was always there, and Stella always helped on every occasion. When she was quite young and I had just gone to live in the big house, I had Stella to wait at my first large dinner party in the enormous dining room, and it was Stella's first dinner party where she hadn't had a butler to tell her what to do. We rehearsed everything beforehand, and all seemed well – the fourteen people sat down and we had our first course, and then in came Stella with a huge dish for the main course with the serving implements on the dish, and there was a hideous pause. I caught my breath and realised that all was well except Stella had forgotten to put round the plates. This we managed to turn into a very funny occasion and the situation was quickly repaired. Stella went from strength to strength and helped at christenings, birthdays and weddings and she is part of the history of Uppark. Stella worked right through her life without pause until almost the day before she died, and she died quite suddenly. As I write this, it is not so long ago, and she had the most wonderful funeral at the village church in Harting. The church was packed with the old village, the people who had always lived there, most of whom were

Stella's relations. This was just how a funeral should be – full of friends and family and flowers everywhere, even on the floor; banks and banks of flowers, and her husband led the singing of the hymn *All Things Bright and Beautiful*, which nearly lifted the roof. After the funeral, there was the most mammoth tea in the village and it seemed as if everyone must have baked and made of their very best. It was all a very fitting tribute to Stella.

Some of the people in the village all those years ago were reputed to look like Sir Harry – and looking at him in early portraits when he certainly sowed wild oats, it is possible. When Emma Hamilton lived at Uppark and he kept going off to London, she had affairs in the village, and it was when she became pregnant that he threw her out, so no doubt village life was entered into from the big house in various ways.

After beginning married life at Uppark, Richard and I moved for a year to a minute cottage in North Wales, where he was to do a spell on a dairy farm. He already had a few Guernsey cows and a cowman at Uppark and wanted to learn more. This cottage was so small that when the removal men arrived, they said, 'Cor, you've got a dolls' house 'ere,' and had to saw our bed in half to get it in. We were very happy there and Richard worked hard with a dairy farmer. His favourite aunt lived near, and was kind, and we had many friends. Our first baby was born in July 1949. Harriet Sarah. She was so small she was like a most beautiful doll, but she flourished and grew – we took her south to Uppark to be christened. When my father-in-law found out that one of Harriet's godparents was a Catholic, he nearly had a fit. He was an Irish Protestant and Roman Catholics were anathema – after the christening, he did not speak to me for six months.

At this same time my mother-in-law's cousin, to whom she was very attached, died. He was Niall, tenth Duke of Argyll. She was at Inverary Castle for his death and funeral. She arrived back unannounced at Uppark, as we were all at dinner in the large dining room one evening – my father-in-law, Richard, me and a nurse. The double dining-room doors flew open and a dramatic scene was enacted by my mother-in-law, who was like one obsessed. She stood and proclaimed the story of how while the duke was dying she had seen the black winged horseman flying through the night. She had heard the owls hoot nine times and heard the ghost piper. It went on and on. I was stunned – even more stunned when she seemed to touch down and see who was there. Upon seeing the nurse, she said, 'WHO is this?' in such an awful voice – then she promptly said,

'The nurse should be eating upstairs.' This was the beginning of the crossed wires between us. I needed the nurse at that time and she was good so I insisted on going with her and we both had to have meals upstairs – luckily the christening was the next day and I think we left soon after. There was a housekeeper called Mrs Geary who was so loyal to my mother-in-law that she acted as a spy, and all my doings were reported. I once had the misfortune of leaving a book behind after a visit and, terrified of stirring up trouble with my mother-in-law, I wrote to Mrs Geary asking if she could kindly send the book. The next thing I knew was a furious letter from my mother-in-law – Mrs Geary had taken her my letter to say not only was I irresponsible and bad mannered, but ignorant – did I not know how to address housekeepers? Apparently, you did not write 'Dear Mrs G.', 'yours sincerely' you wrote 'Mrs G.' then stated your message! I now can't remember how I should have signed off. Times have changed.

My parents-in-law had been involved in the royal household all their lives. One day during one of our visits to Uppark, the Queen Mother came to lunch. It was realised she always wore peeptoe shoes and would want to see outside the front of the house, which was knee-deep in thistles. Richard had to rise at dawn and with his scythe mow all the front lawn and the Queen Mother did go outside, mercifully without damage to her feet.

My first realisation of a different sense of proportion and the value of things was when I told my mother-in-law that Richard and I were planning to knock two of the cottages together. These cottages had been the deerkeeper's cottage and were intact, older than Uppark itself, but my mother-in-law couldn't stretch her imagination to see her son Richard and me living in cottages. She found this unacceptable and demeaning. A friction was created which became inflamed through the years. If only I had known then what I know now and realised there is always a way of turning a head-on clash of energy into a triangular situation, with higher consciousness as the third point, then conflict ceases. However, this did come about later.

So we moved south again to Uppark into Deerkeeper's Cottage, and there troubles began. Again, it was interesting because the energy of Uppark was then very turbulent and again I met negative energy in my mother-in-law and all her very interesting doings. She was growing saponaria in the garden and using it to restore eighteenth-century fabrics. She introduced me to homeopathy and she was also a very active herbalist. But her obsession with material things was really awesome, I couldn't understand it and this made her terribly difficult and resentful if anyone looked as if they might ever take over from her, or, worse, succeed her. The things that she had owned most of her life she would have to pass on. It's interesting now to see at the end of all this how 'things' really are not what matters to the evolution of the essence of somebody. Anyway my duty and my conscience prompted me to hang on and to survive troubles.

The wonderful event of Emma's birth at Deerkeepers in July 1951 brought much happiness – Richard so loved his children and was with them a lot of the time. So many children now are utterly deprived of this precious gift of time and attention from parents. Why have children if you can't give them enough love? So there we had two beautiful little girls, admired by many, particularly our neighbour and friend the artist Paul Maze. Paul was such a support to us. Richard painted a lot and learned much from him and we are the fortunate owners of many of his pictures. It was hard though to make friends under my mother-in-law's eye. Our cottage was beginning to seem too small so we made plans to go further away.

During this time we became interested in the work of Rudolf Steiner. We were pioneers of ideas for organic farming and studied his philosophy not only on farming but on a way of life – though we felt isolated in our ideas. Richard and I were visited by Sir George Trevelyan and Lady Eve Balfour, and we all discussed organic farming at Uppark. Sir George founded the Soil Association, now the hallmark of quality organic food everywhere. Many years later, these harmonious ideas were to become more acceptable, but at this time people thought we were a bit batty.

In 1954, we moved away from Uppark, though we kept in close contact with the farm, to a pretty farmhouse near Andover called Bransbury. We moved with the Guernsey herd and Bob. Bob was an essential person and I mention more about him later.

Just after moving in to the house, in March 1954, Sophie was born, causing much excitement and rejoicing. A nice, kind nanny arrived and took care of all three children. Nanny was a great stabiliser – a rock – and whenever Richard had an asthma attack which necessitated an ambulance and hospitals, or when we went abroad, Nanny was always there for them.

Bransbury had a charming, rather secret garden surrounded by a wall with a thatched edge on top. This was a very old craft and like the house had been there many years, but the place had a history of disasters –

accidents, divorces, diseases, deaths. It was here that I began to learn more about dowsing and different earth energies, some of which seemed to move in lines, like good or bad streams. There were negative energies going through this farm and it was right that we later moved from here. Though we were very happy, Richard had more and more severe attacks. I lived on the edge of a precipice, my moods swinging from calm to panic. In between attacks, Richard was the strong farmer who enjoyed shooting and all normal activities, then suddenly he would become really ill. He seemed to hold off an attack as long as I was with him but after three days and nights I could hold out no longer. He felt the healing from my hands, though I didn't realise this until later. At this time, I took Richard to a healer who was a very remarkable, eccentric lady called Lillian Young. She, through the laying on of hands, could help sickness and disease. We also went to another healer who said to me, 'You should be doing this.' It was said so factually I felt astounded that it was possible that I could do such a thing myself it was awesome.

To imagine through one's hands such power could stream, that it could change the state of another's being, was amazing. I found I could help Richard but through the years his asthma, which had taken a terrible toll, got worse. I could not help enough. Bad attacks always ended up with ghastly journeys in ambulances to hospitals. But the wonderful knowledge of being able to use my hands like this changed my life. It became a huge outlet for this feeling I had while nursing that I could do something. Later, it became a very important part of my life and subsequently many other people's too. Since healing through touch opens people's inner eyes, many of them found they could heal too. We are told this in the early, unexpurgated writings of the gospels (Thomas) and in the earliest Christian manuscripts and the Nag Hammadi papers.

Day-to-day life at Bransbury was happy. Richard farming, shooting, me with children and garden, Bob with the Guernsey herd. Bob – I always called him the right hand man in my life and later on he would be the whole family's right hand man – has seen three generations of us through.

When Richard and I married, and were living at Uppark in 1950, Richard had a few Guernsey cows and a Cockney cowman and needed more help. He enlisted a Latvian from the local camp where displaced people were living. In fact he engaged two Latvians, but one soon fell out as he used to go on binges which made him unable to turn up for work. And the other was Bob – Robert Senbergs – but with the usual English non-attempt to speak any foreign word or name, he was called

Bob and Mr Bob by the younger generations and others. He was a remarkable person who learned to adapt to English life largely because of his previous country life in Latvia and on his home farm, and through his understanding of nature and animals. He learned a wonderful special form of English which was a cross between Cockney and broad Sussex. I related to him in a partnership that never failed – when Richard was ill in hospital he only wanted to see Bob and to hear about the cows. As time went by Bob took over the herd which was to become well-known as the Uppark pedigree Guernsey herd, and the largest milk-producing herd in Hampshire. Bob understood Richard's silent ways, it seemed. He would talk for ages about cows, hardly receiving an answer – maybe a smile or laugh, but Bob never needed answers. He just knew. When we went to live in Switzerland, Richard kept in close touch with Bob, who carried on in his unfailing way. After a while, in 1983, I decided to sell the herd and give up Bransbury. I was by then living half in London and half at Uppark with three children all at different schools. The herd was making good money but I sometimes have a feeling about some move I should make or something I should do quite without reason. This has always been difficult to convey to businessmen and people working on an intellectual level. However, this time I was trusted by my professional advisors and the herd went for sale. Bob took this seemingly in his usual calm way. He, like me, had dealt with shocks and big readjustments in life. The hardest thing was the fear of giving up what had been his home for years – his cottage at Bransbury. When Bob first arrived, the farming people in the adjoining cottages in the Bransbury hamlet would not cook his dinner for him as he was foreign, so I did. Gradually, they adopted him and when he left he seemed to be tearing out part of their lives by his going like the roots of a tree which had been growing there through the years. He came back to Uppark where he had started and moved into his stable flat. He brought some calves with him to rear and I think this helped him to readjust. The family grew up all around him, always knowing Mr Bob would fix it or know what to do about it or how to handle a natural disaster ... but then for the first time Bob was not himself. There seemed to be lots of small things going wrong – his way of expressing that he felt unsettled, I guess.

Always I have been advised and have consulted an astrologer for myself and people with whom I had dealings. It helped me to understand them on a deeper level. Bob was no exception – he is Cancer and people born under Cancer hate moves. The possible compensation was frequent listeners as Bob liked a sounding board – all the family were around. He joined them on high days and holidays, for Christmas lunch, Easter Sunday and eggs and other feast days. I was often elsewhere, but he was always most loyal and always in touch. Nothing was done without referral to me, 'the boss', as I was called. Then we received quite a shock – Bob's wife, whom he had not seen since the war, was arriving to stay from Latvia. We had made attempts before, but behind the Iron Curtain communication was difficult. We got permission for a visit for her in 1988. Everyone held their breath. She spoke no word of English. Bob was exhausted by all the translating, shopping, explaining etc. She went back after two weeks, but in 1990 the Iron Curtain came down and after several more visits she arrived to stay properly. What a marvellous, loyal, brave person, and Bob was so happy. It was not until the last year or two that Bob was with us that he and I talked about his life, especially after he had been back to Latvia on visits, and about my life. He knew about the healing work I was doing – there was somehow never a need to explain very much – about the various family problems which he always seemed instinctively to have guessed. He assessed the grandchildren very accurately and seemed to relate to each one in their own way. Bob's life had always been as a cattle farmer in the most Godly way of country living. In old age (he is the same age as me) he pieced together what was left of life. In 2000, he went back to Latvia, and once more on his own home ground made good his house in the country and stacked his famous woodpile for hard winters. He and his wife live happily ever after and this really is a fairy tale. We were in constant touch until Bob left us all in 2000, a year of hope and change everywhere.

While we lived at Bransbury, we went abroad from time to time. One year we decided to go to Spain to the Costa Brava, which at that time was almost unknown to most holidaymakers. In the suburbs of Barcelona people were living in caves. They were really poor, their children had almost no clothes and almost no food. Franco changed this but change takes time. In the country, life was easier but behind the times compared to the rest of the Continent. We drove through France to the Pyrenees to the highest point on the map where there was a frontier post. When we got there, no way would the Guardia let us go on. No foreign cars were at that time allowed into Spain unless every number and part of the engine was registered and checked out again later. Despite much pleading, for it was by then a wet and windy night on the mountain, we were blocked. So back we drove to the foothills and on to the main frontier and having acquired the necessary documents into Spain, we finally went. We both fell in love with Spain. It had a most deeply calming effect – a feeling of solidarity and a most wonderful climate – dry above all, and Richard was well. We drove to a large fishing village called Cadaques, then completely unspoilt by commercialism – it was a good place to paint and Richard as always painted and lost himself in it. One day at the bus stop in the village square we saw an extraordinary looking man whom we talked with. He had an enormous black moustache, a long black cloak with a red satin lining, knee-high green leather boots and a glass walking stick with coloured barley sugar twists inside, which he twirled about. He was very gregarious and said we should go along the beach to Port Liligat and see his work. Along the beach we found a shack surrounded by the most extraordinary sort of shapes and figures – they made me stare, they were most arresting and made one pause and think – do we all see exactly the same things as we think we see? This man became very famous indeed – Salvador Dali. I came years later to be fascinated by his painting and his way of waking people up to a sense of seeing they maybe did not know they had.

We went on from Cadaques down the beautiful Costa Brava until we reached a tiny village with one inn called Calella – little did we know the part in our lives Calella was to play – we both loved it and stayed at the inn, which had a beautiful arched terrace on to the beach within yards of the sea. The sea wall was always occupied by rows of fishermen, for this was a fishing village whose male population went out at night in their boats with their nets to fish for their living. They sat on the wall in the sun by day and seemed so content, so still and really happy. Each night they took their lives in their hands – the sea can be cruel and they were as close to death as life. What wonderful people – real people living so close to nature unspoilt by modern materialism and technology, so-called progress. There people were deeply religious and superstitious, and festivals and holy days were rigorously kept. Church prayers and dancing and drinking and eating all went together. The dancing lasted all day when it was a festival. They danced a kind of reel, like the Scots, to very Moorish music called the Sadana. People joined in and danced until they almost fell out and another would join in – such a feeling of communal sharing and compassion. Of course we never imagined Richard would die here some years later but we did decide if he was too ill to live at Uppark we would live there. We even looked at a pretty pink house. So then back to Bransbury and our children.

CHAPTER FOUR

Travels and Losing Richard

St Tropez – Madeira – Mont d'Or – move to
Switzerland – Spain – Richard's death

ANOTHER JOURNEY we took was to the south of France to St Tropez back then almost empty of tourists. Those who were there were rich, chic yacht owners who ate in the most expensive restaurants, but it was calm and unhassled. As it was not really for us, we moved to St Maxime, a charming, old-fashioned seaside place reminiscent of Victorian England. There, Richard painted and painted in the lovely sun and dry air. At that time money restrictions for English people were very stringent so we moved into a very cheap pre-booked pension in a small place further on. We were very pleased with it and Richard went out on the balcony and sat back while I settled in, but he came back in a state because the balcony had no privacy and there was a naked lady lying next door. Upon further inspection of balcony and beach we discovered we were in a nudist colony – so in haste I had to re-pack and smuggle the cases back into our car before announcing to the Madame that we had to leave – naturally this didn't happen without ruffled feathers, but was achieved in the end. My best memory of this visit was the forests of mimosa trees, all out in clouds of such a dazzling bright yellow.

En route for home, we spent a day at a magical beach with miles of silver sand and the largest and most beautiful shells I have ever seen. It was Ste Marie de la Mer. This was said to be the place where Mary, Mary Magdalene and St Joseph of Aramathea landed in their coracle on their way to Glastonbury. All the gypsies from everywhere meet here once a year for their festival of The Saint Maries. They go into the sea to be cleansed. We didn't stay here as there was only a small inn, and it was a mosquito area, but somehow it had a holy magic about it. One could imagine the holy family arriving there and experiencing this atmosphere. I visited Ste Marie de la Mer some years later; it had been treated by pesticides of many kinds which had exterminated all mosquitoes and whatever else. It had been sanitised (or sterilised) and there were miles of concrete blocks of hotels and no shells – the beaches were very crowded with people. I thought of the sheer beauty we came across on that first visit.

All these experiences of light and colour made me find a new kind of inner dimension of space which could be called upon in times of stress – perhaps a glimpse into the state of mind meditation leads to, and beyond to heavenly colours. This would lead me into healing work later in life. Then, the return to Bransbury, farm and children, all held together by Bob and Nanny.

One autumn Richard had been very ill and we decided, on the doctor's advice, that we must try and get some sun. Where could we go where we could be sure to get the sun at Christmas? Then my marvellous Granny, who for her day and age had been really quite a traveller, suggested Madeira. I'm ashamed to say I had almost never heard of Madeira but I knew it was a Portuguese island somewhere off Africa. Unfortunately we didn't gather very much travel information about it before we went, but we packed up and off we set in a large liner. On leaving Southampton we moved into a cabin. I had never been on such a ship before, and we unpacked and it all seemed very nice. We set sail and to my horror that evening I realised that this was like a floating hotel, where we were expected to dress up in evening dress for dinner every night and there was a tremendous thing about where you sat and whose table you sat on and so on. I seem to remember we did for a short spell find two very congenial old friends but they were getting off after a day or two at one of the stops. Anyway we enjoyed their company for a bit but Richard was really not well. We then got into very bad weather. This was appalling. All night and all day this huge liner tossed and worst of all was the fearful creaking. I felt absolutely certain it was going to bust into pieces and there was a lot of banging, china crashing, and one of the old stewards who had done the journey backwards and forwards almost all his life told me afterwards that it was the roughest storm he had ever sailed through in the Bay of Biscay. I survived, up to a point. Poor Richard was terribly seasick so he spent the whole time lying in bed and he wasn't well anyway. Eventually we arrived at a port off Spain called Vigo. I knew that if we were allowed ashore, however seasick we were, we that we would be OK once our feet touched the land. It's a very strange thing, seasickness. So we were given our passports and told that we had three hours. Richard stayed put. I was only too thankful to disembark and dive off into this really rather attractive little town, built on a hill with narrow cobbled streets. It was so marvellous after all those days at sea that I felt quite revived. I wandered along and went into the market and into the local shops. I suppose I had gone really quite a long way when quite suddenly I heard to my sickening horror the hooting of a liner. I thought I had made a terrible mistake and the liner was about to set sail without me. I have run fast in times of crisis but this was certainly one of them. I tore down the hill with panting heart and sweat pouring down my face to arrive at the gangway where we embarked to be told simply not to worry, there was still another two hours and that the hoot I heard had been something quite different. Oh dear, but anyway, that fright was enough to get me on board again and on we went sailing towards Madeira. We finally arrived to stay in a very well-known hotel that I think must have been absolutely the first ever built for tourists in Edwardian days called Reids. It was charmingly old-fashioned with really good service and people who were used to old-fashioned manners and a nice way of doing things. We had a great welcome. Little did I know that the biggest family on the island who grew the Madeira wine, and probably owned Reids Hotel, were relations of my future son-in-law. It is extraordinary how history goes. He must have been a very small boy at the time, and I don't remember meeting him then. The thing I do remember about Madeira is that we were there over Christmas, and I remember so well going to church on Christmas Day and the whole church being adorned with gardenias. The shiny dark green leaves and the wonderful white flowers and the smell were one of my strongest impressions.

We were very kindly entertained to lunch by the Blandy family, who were relations of my son-in-law, and after that things really did not go according to plan. Richard, instead of getting better, got worse; I think there could have been a number of factors but nobody had told us that Madeira is a volcanic island and volcanic areas are very often damp and, of course, damp was the worst thing for him. It was warm at Christmas, I remember swimming but it certainly wasn't hot and Richard spent a lot of time in bed. I made friends with a most charming old couple, two very distinguished people who made all the difference to my life – Sir John and Lady Salmon. I used to have dinner with them in the evening and Lady Salmon was a great swimmer. We would set off and swim together. She was most charmingly Victorian and she wore a bathing-suit that I had only seen in photographs, rather like a child's bloomers – very voluminous, down to the knee, gathered there with elastic, black, and on her head she wore something that resembled a black mob cap into which she tucked her beautiful hair. As she lowered herself into the water enormous bubbles arose. She looked like a huge black balloon going down but my word, she could swim. I think she had been quite a champion in her day. Richard got still worse and we had to have a doctor. Now this doctor was a very special person, a German doctor called Belmonte. History did not relate how or why he had left Germany, but I suspect he was a refugee from his country. He was not only a very brilliant man but he was a very good-hearted person, a real beacon of light in the darkness. He always had time to talk and to really sit down and discuss interesting things, thereby distracting us from the rather agonising situation of the asthma attacks. Our money ran out. We were not allowed by the government to take very much money out of the country and the hotel room booking came to an end, so very uncomfortable arrangements had to be made and we were moved into an annexe in the garden where we stayed, as it turned out for nearly two months. The doctor felt that Richard really was so ill that he ought to see the children, and then followed an anxious few days because ringing up from Madeira was an almost impossible feat in those days and, as always, real friends come forward in moments of crisis.

On the sunbathing ledge, lying on straw palisades we would greet a whole variety of people, most of them fairly well off. Among them was a very tough little man who was an absolute king of a vast business empire which made carpets, and of all the people that I had made friends with he was the most stalwart and staunch and helpful. He managed somehow to telephone, to organise, to do everything that needed to be done, and the crisis passed over and we decided it was better not to fly Nanny and such small children out to Madeira. Landing at that time in Madeira was quite a hazard too. It rather depended on the weather and people were put into a boat from a seaplane to land. Anyway, eventually when Richard was well enough, that trouble was over.

The following year we decided to go to France for Richard to do a water cure. Now someone had told me about these wonderful cures done at spas all over the world, but mainly in Europe. I had heard about a place called the Mont d'Or, in the middle of France, the Dordogne, and here out of the volcanic rocks sprang many different springs and the water was different from each spring, with different minerals and these had very curative properties. The Romans knew about this and they built wonderful baths and means by which people could benefit and be cured from the waters. The Mont d'Or had grown up around these springs and there were hundreds of hotels. Still using the Roman baths but with modern tiled additions, were the baths in which people soaked, they were sprayed with it, they stood in rooms filled with the steam from it and they drank it endlessly until they were absolutely impregnated with this water, which in this particular place was for lungs and breathing difficulties. After three weeks, Richard felt terribly tired and looking at his paintings one can really see from the dark, gloomy colours he used, how unwell he must have felt. He was breathing very much better, in fact he really was amazingly better and I feel sure that had he done this earlier in life he would probably still be with us. The cure, to be really effective, had to be done three years running and very sadly, before we managed the second year, he had died.

But there was a wonderful place, a bit less high, called Bourboule which is the place for children. When I got back to England, and much later, I tried to enthuse my doctor to send people to these marvellous watering places and use them, but the English medical establishment was not interested in healing water, though it had been used successfully for thousands of years. While we were at Mont d'Or, two of our oldest and greatest friends, Christopher and Anne Scott, who actually lived in Scotland but who also went to Italy quite a lot, were motoring across France, back from Italy, and on their way were good enough to make the journey round to come and see us there. These friends have all through my life acted as catalysts when a move was going to be a good idea, and when someone else besides us had to suggest something. They said, 'You cannot possibly go back to Uppark and go on having these terrible asthma attacks, why don't you go to live in Switzerland where there are wonderful doctors and wonderful air?' Richard adored the mountains; he climbed and skied and loved everything about them. So as we were away, and emotionally detached from our normal surroundings, it was much easier to discuss this. We decided it would be a good idea to let our house and go to Switzerland to try it out. It was exactly the right idea at the right time; they were the right people in the right place, because when one is detached it is very much easier to see things in a different perspective, and somehow I think Richard and I knew that the time had come to decide he was no longer able to live in England. This was a terrible decision to have to make, and we hadn't really even discussed it, but we both knew and these dear good friends came up with all sorts of remarks and ideas which made it possible to discuss a move abroad, to somewhere Richard would be well. They knew people all over the place. While we were there we freely and happily planned the idea of going to live in Switzerland. So by the time we got back to England we really had decided to get on with it. I have been so grateful through the years to these friends. Richard said, very bravely, 'Oh well, I'll go and see how I get on and if I'm better, you can join me.' I said, 'No way. Where you go, we go.'

So we packed up. The girls were three, four and five. I bought them each a rucksack, a tiny one, into which they put what they called their precious things. You know it is very important for everyone, whatever age, for their own security, to have something which they possess which to them spells comfort, whether it is a teddy bear, or pictures or later in life china or whatever a person can identify with and base themselves on. They each had their little packs on their back and besides their own precious thing had toothbrushes and night things. This in the end proved a very good idea because they would travel more than I had foreseen. Returning from Mont d'Or to Bransbury, I had to set to – I let the house and packed up. The greatest difficulty at this time was money. The Labour government would only allow medical allowance for Richard abroad, not for us. So I and three babies were going to have to live on his allowance – £5 a day – very little! We would have to live in the simplest way. Nanny left us to get married and the plan was to have an au pair girl to help. So into our lives came Brigitta. She was Swedish and I knew she would understand life in the mountains and snow. She was a real stalwart, splendid, Nordic character with blonde hair plaited and coiled round her head. She was so merry and strong and nice. The plan was to pack the trunk and send Brigitta ahead to arrive in a chalet I had taken in a village where I had skied before the war. It was high above a Swiss valley called Chesière near Villars, where I knew of a very good doctor so that made it feel quite safe.

Meanwhile, while I was packing Richard stayed in London where he went to a school of art in Camberwell to try and do some drawing. His paintings were seen by a very famous man, the principal. He produced his watercolours and this man said, 'I don't think I want to touch them, they are beautiful and you have your own style, so I suggest you just do drawing.' And he did. Richard was terribly funny about it, because he stayed at his club, Brookes's, which is a very smart, well established gentlemen's club in St James's with the most wonderful hall porter, a great character called Newman. Richard always wore a bowler hat and an umbrella and a stiff collar when in London, done in those days, but how to arrive dressed for art school? He told the most wonderful story of how he had to leave Brookes's in his London clothes and change on top of a bus into cords and cotton shirt. This sort of thing never worried him. He found it all very funny and I'm sure everyone at art school got on very well and loved him. He was not a communicator, he was a very closed up person, but he took things in, and sometimes when he spoke he did it off the top of his head from sheer nerves; at other times he said something either very funny or very much to the point. Perhaps a lot of us talk too much; I think I must have made up for him.

Richard returned from London. Disaster pursued us because when all was ready for Switzerland, we were to be there, I think, for Christmas or in December, all the family got flu, so Brigitta went ahead with the trunk. As soon as the girls and Richard were able to stand up, we set off and arrived in Geneva, then got on a small train to the station in the valley where we changed to the mountain train, by which time it was snowing very hard in the encroaching darkness. It could have been exciting but I will confess to being apprehensive. When we arrived at the stop at the top in the mountain village, the stationmaster came forward and greeted us with appalling news. Brigitta had stepped out of the train and broken her leg very badly, and she was in the hospital in Geneva – a bad beginning. Somehow we got the village porter to get the trunk on to a toboggan with the rest of our luggage and we reached our new abode. This was a very different life altogether. The next morning I simply couldn't believe my eyes. The snow was up to the windows and I had to dig my way out of the front door. However, the sun was shining and the sky was blue. Everything was beautiful and so I left my three little girls to play in the snow outside, but this proved to be unwise. I did not know the mountains, and the next day Sophie was terribly ill with sunstroke. She became delirious. Luckily the doctor had been warned we were coming and he was perfectly marvellous and attentive, and Sophie got over it, and like all Swiss doctors, he had excellent remedies.

From then, on we began life in the mountains. The name of this place was Villars. In fact the place where we lived was the old village below Villars called Chesière, and it had enormous charm. We lived in the first floor flat of a very big old chalet. The flat actually belonged to a Swiss musician called Souttermeister, who let us have it on fairly cheap rent as long as he could have it back for the summer. We had a really happy time there. We lived like peasants for most of the time and had a bit of help when we felt we could afford it. Two out of three children went to

Switzerland: Richard in the snow

day school. One of the girls we had to help us really was the personification of Heidi, she was quite charming; blonde plaits and singing all day long. She didn't mind what she did, and worked like an ox, teaching Sophie her first French words on the way. In the spring, when the snow melted, Heidi had to leave us to go down and fetch her father's cows and bring them up to graze in the mountains. This was a tremendous festival in all the mountain villages; you heard the cows by their huge bells coming up, and they also had wonderful flower wreaths around their necks. They plodded their way up the mountain to the new grass where they would spend the summer. Heidi called in on her way to see us with a very excited grin on her face and a box, and in the box, to my horror and the delight of the girls, was a kitten, which didn't stay very long, I seem to remember!

When Richard was well, he was a marvellous skier, and sometimes I went with him, unable to keep up, but he was always terribly good-natured and slowed down to stay with me. Curiously, when you live abroad, your really good, dear friends who you see at home but not often, come and stay with you and you see them properly and under special circumstances. Several of our friends did this and it was wonderful.

The big day was Sunday because abroad Sunday is the day to go and eat out. Swiss Families treat eating out as real occasions, so along with the rest, we went to a local restaurant. As we were quite poor and they gave large portions, it seemed not too embarrassing and was quite the done thing on the Continent – we used to have three portions and five plates, much to the children's amusement. There, it made absolute sense but it was very embarrassing later in England when the girls and I would ask for two menus and four plates and the waiter looked rather surprised.

We really didn't have very many other outings but there were one or two frightening occasions when I had to get the car out as the snow was melting, though the roads were terribly slippery, and go down to Geneva to the children's dentist. My real absolute horror was driving down the mountains, down the hairpin bends – I suffer from vertigo and it has been far worse since this experience. I have always been frightened of mountains. I am not happy in them. I find them very awesome, frightening and overwhelming, and it was extraordinary in that deep winter, the longest winter that many old people could recall. The snow actually covered our chalet up to the top windows and in the morning when one opened the door, there was a solid block of snow. It gave one an idea of how it must be to have an avalanche fall on you – to be in a space where of course it was dark and sound seemed to be deadened, quite frightening, but of course help came. Besides us having to dig and dig a way out like rabbits, there arrived from the village a very efficient snow plough. This was never more than hours before there was an entrance and an exit, but somehow snow is so utterly relentless, making whatever you do seem a scratch on the surface. Anyway, when it melted and the spring came and wonderful flowers emerged, I felt rather differently about the mountains. There were many charming local customs that we were privileged to see, and from each one something was learned. A way of communal life and communal celebration which we seem to have lost in England. We have certainly lost it in urban areas – people no longer relate to the time of year, the tides and the stars and moon; with the turn of each season comes a natural festival and it is sad that we treat one day much as the next and the next, as just ordinary.

There was a great New Year festival when all the skiers, almost everyone in the village, went up to the top of the mountain where there was a good deal of hot wine, *Glüwein*, or something delicious and in the dark they would hold burning torches and ski all the way down in spectacular procession. It was also a great appreciation of the magnificence and power of the mountains.

I remembered these incidents of being snowed in when years later I lived in Barnes in London and it snowed deeply. My neighbours each came out and shovelled and swept it away outside their own houses; I was not very strong so mine had to be left. This would never have happened in Chesière – all natural disasters were automatically shared and you swept your neighbours' snow away with the whole street participating.

We decided to go back in the summer to Calella in Spain. Everything about it was gorgeous and then unspoilt, and we decided as the girls were with us to take a house. We drove over the Pyrenees, and it was wonderfully dry air, so Richard was well. Of course the Spaniards were not geared up at all for tourism in those days, and their idea and our idea of renting were totally different. By correspondence I had rented a fisherman's cottage in a row, and apart from the number of rooms that was all I knew about it. It was two down and three up or the other way round, and one was expected, like all the fishermen's wives, to cook on a charcoal grill out in the street. This I could not get to grips with at all, and somehow this was intimated and overnight a woman appeared who bought the fish in the mornings and grilled them, and produced our food, cleaned the house and all else. We were very surprised to find there were hardly any lights in the place and we had to do nearly everything before the sun set. Richard and I walked around the village with delight, and in two or three days he was so well, and it seemed such a happy place that we thought we could move there, and a governess for the children was possible. Richard loved the light there and painted and painted. A few days later we celebrated Emma's birthday. Somehow we managed a cake and candles and some presents, and that was an excitement, and then we went to the beach. There had been a storm the night before and there were Men o' War jellyfish everywhere, which looked fiercer than normal jellyfish, brightly coloured and spiny. We did avoid many, but Richard was actually stung by one. At the time it didn't seem anything much, though he did say it had made him very asthmatic in North Africa when he was stung. But he wasn't, and he seemed all right, then the next day he was very much not all right and a terrible attack came on quite quickly. I ran up the road. There was only one telephone in the village, a communal telephone behind a bead curtain, and with great difficulty I did get through to a doctor to come. Though the message got through, it was obvious that Richard was really very ill, and he died suddenly before the doctor arrived.

As Richard died, I saw a light rising up above him in a huge spiral –

Calella

like a kind of rainbow, mostly silvery blue – I have seen this light since when a man died in hospital once and a priest and I had been there to give healing. I have seen lights in various places at various times, but when Richard died I was very conscious of it. Somehow I felt that what I had always believed about death and how our souls leave our bodies had been confirmed. I knew for sure that what I had suspected actually was. This light as on many later occasions was what gave me an unearthly strength.

While Richard's asthma attack was coming on, I had sent a girl to look after the children and had said, 'Don't come back until I send for you.' The awful result was that when I did send for them it was after Richard had died and they had been on the beach for many hours and Harriet was badly sunburnt. I hope she is no longer scarred and it wasn't so bad as to make her ill. I had to have time to compose myself after this trauma. The doctor was very nice but there was nothing he could do so he went away again. There was a wonderful old fisherwoman next door, and they are the people to be with on these occasions – they are used to death and they accept and take it as part of being. Though we had not a word in common, she did what was necessary and she was just there. Then the first thing of course that the village did was to send for the priest. The priest walked into the house and said, 'Are you Roman Catholic?' and when I said no he simply turned around and walked away. This was, I fear, not untypical of the Catholicism to be found in many areas at that time, not only in Spain. And after a day, the nuns in the convent at Palafrugell took Richard's body and he was there in the most beautiful place in great peace, until the funeral two days later. The nuns were very beautiful and I used to go and visit them each year, and thank them. They really did practise Christianity in the best way.

The worst part in all this was trying to call England. I think I probably rang my sister-in-law Anne, who was very close to Richard. Telephoning from Spain then was a mammoth job, particularly from a Catalan village. As soon as we got through and they heard English, everything was dropped and disconnected and it seemed the same at the British end – in those days it seemed we were very far from home in Spain. So Anne, in her wonderful efficient way took things in hand, having alerted the Spanish ambassador, and came flying out, but the consul from Barcelona was required at the scene and had disappeared without trace on holiday – he was rather badly caught out, poor man. Our great friends the landlords of the bar next door were salt of the earth people and supported me a lot. According to custom, I was not allowed out of the house for three days, which I respected. The house was small and enclosed and the three days were perhaps a very good thing as I really did have time to collect myself. There is much to be said for old habits and old customs and they are a teaching for a very good reason.

Our marvellous cook, Belen, went off to the local town and bought me several mourning dresses; the only suitable one was grey and white checked gingham, and I remember wearing it day in, day out until we eventually left Spain about a month later.

A most extraordinary thing happened as I was calling England with the news of Richard's death, someone in the village fetched a lady who spoke English and it transpired she was a most charming person called Blanche Hanbury-Tracey who kept a guest house. She was immediately a link with everyone and everything and spoke fluent Spanish. So she helped me but was very busy with her guest house so she said, 'Listen, I've got a girlfriend staying with me, I'm sure she will come along,' and the girlfriend was Virginia, a cousin of my best friend from when I first married and went to Uppark! Virginia's cousin lived in Harting and was called Iris Cos and she was the most wonderful friend through the years there. Virginia was marvellous and stayed with me a great deal of the day, helping with the children and anything else.

There was not very much I could do except arrange the funeral and it had to be held very quickly, the custom in Mediterranean countries. It had its difficulties because we were not Catholic, but there was a charming cemetery attached to the Catholic cemetery in a town some miles away called San Feliux. The really nice thing about it was that it was opposite the bullring where people enjoyed themselves so much. It seemed right to have the two extremes. Meanwhile the Consul had tracked down the Bishop of Gibraltar who happened to be on holiday in a village just down the coast.

Poor Bishop, he had gone away and taken a flat above the greengrocer's in the village, and he was fetched to take the funeral I can only say that it was my greatest good fortune that he was the person who was with me at that time because he was a very holy man, and such a comfort to me. We drove to the funeral in a small, enclosed van, not a grand hearse at all, and people brought lovely flowers, and so did I. The Bishop turned to me and said, 'You know, my dear, you will never be lonely if you learn to be alone.' This was the most important thing, and has always stuck with me. If one can learn to be alone at all times, even with people, it makes no difference, you become a whole person. A wonderful man.

So Richard's grave is there among the olive trees, which I love so much, with a beautiful piece of marble hewn from the local quarry, on his grave. Spaniards are sensitive about these things; besides being artistic they are very thoughtful, and I was taken by the stonemason to the quarry to choose from the huge blocks there. I thought this was very touching. So there is his grave and I have always planted rosemary there. I haven't been for many years now, but we all used to go. I don't feel it makes any difference actually where one's body is buried. The grave remains maybe as a symbol of a person, but I believe that the essence of people goes on and goes on everywhere like light and air, so that the actual place only matters to us, who are left here.

Before we left for home, another miracle happened. On the beach I was introduced to some English people on holiday and they turned out to be friends of the couple to whom we had let Bransbury on a two-year open lease. Our tenants were newlyweds and had just settled into the house and decorated. But when their friends told them about my loss, they immediately from the goodness of their hearts offered to move out so the girls and I could return to our home at Bransbury – I hope all concerned were rewarded for their generosity later in life.

I certainly accepted their offer as I knew it would be easier for the children at home, and I also had the yoke of Uppark permanently on my shoulders and I knew I had to look at this situation. About a month later we went home, and that moment was one of the hardest. It was just kind of leaving everything behind and in a way I felt I was leaving Richard behind, though deep down that is not what I believe, but it was very hard nevertheless.

I really loved Spain. I loved Spain before he died, and when we were there together, and I think from the moment I met it, and my love has always continued. I go back to Spain quite often and every time it is like going home and leaving

Travel in Spain

always makes me sad. It is a beautiful country, but it is the very deep feeling, it is a healing feeling, of immense depth, strength and steadiness it gives. Richard's death was a tremendous test of faith. It is hard to describe in words but it was the most wonderful feeling of confirmation in my belief in spite of the appalling shock – the shock, grief and physical bereavement really came later and this I had to suppress very much because I felt the girls completely relied on my reactions. I should really have grieved more openly, but at the time I didn't think it right, with my 'stiff upper lip' upbringing.

So when I had to tell the children that Richard had died, I said Daddy had gone away and we wouldn't actually see him any more, but he had turned into light and so we knew he was everywhere and would always be around. So light was the word I stressed. Then Sophie, who was not a person who simply accepted things, said, 'But Mummy what happens at night?' and so, lost for another thought, I said, 'Oh, he's one of the stars.' So that night we looked up and we decided we saw Daddy as one of the stars and that was acceptable at the time. Things went on and these thoughts remained in their minds. Then years later, Sophie's boarding-school rang up during the first term in quite a fuss, saying, 'We find Sophie knows nothing – she is completely uncommunicative and the last time she did speak she was very voluble and argumentative with her geography teacher.' So I got in the car and went down to the school and found from Sophie that her teacher had asked if anyone knew what stars were – bright Sophie had replied, 'Yes, I know, one star is my Daddy,' and the uncompassionate teacher had disagreed and slapped her down. This shook Sophie's faith, and there were questions which the teacher couldn't answer, so it was a good thing I went, and afterwards she was much happier at school.

After a year settled in at Bransbury, I felt I wanted to take the children back to Villars and collect my thoughts and tidy some business, so we went skiing. Before I'd been in the hotel twenty-four hours, the village policeman came along with an unpaid parking fine summons we had left a year before – how typically Swiss!

CHAPTER FIVE

Meals on Wheels

Jean de Wykerslooth – Uppark – Meg – Sir Malcolm Sargent – London – meals on wheels – Uppark Stables – Greece – Rhodesia – Egypt – Rhodesia again – my father's death and the UDI

I WAS INTRODUCED AT THE HOTEL to a most charming Belgian, Jean de Wykerslooth – so strange that he too was there with his children as his wife had died in Villars at the same time as Richard. We became very good friends; we were both terribly sad, but young and with children to keep going for – we shared tears and laughter and our children for many years. After fifty years, he is still the dearest friend. Jean was a deeply spiritual person and we shared thoughts at soul level though he was a Roman Catholic and sometimes we had disagreements. Sometimes he came to Bransbury and was highly amused by the English way of life – he could not understand a point-to-point in the country, or in the summer,

strange and boring cricket matches in the village. We both enjoyed food, and being French he was a brilliant cook. One year we shared a seaside villa in France with some friends of mine joining us. All our children had such fun, and we did laugh even though we felt much inner pain, so it was good. Sometimes I stayed with him in Paris, which I knew well anyway, but after several years, I had to make a decision as Jean wanted us to marry which was a huge dilemma – there is a huge divide between the French and English character and way of

Patmos

life. The French work hard to keep to their own severe standards. They are much tougher than us and in Jean's milieu did not make allowances as the English do. The only times Jean and I argued and got very cross were over our children – small things like Jean admonishing mine for not putting their hands on the dinner table, and me his for doing the opposite! And over bedtimes – my very young children went to bed after a small supper and long before my evening began. Jean's children stayed up late for adult dinner which I found tiresome. I also had a clear warning that like many Continental families, his parents might come and live with us when they grew old, and in England we are independent of our elders. I didn't feel I had the stamina to keep up with the frenetic social life, fun as it was, and most of all I didn't know if I could manage to keep Uppark on while living in Paris. So, sadly, marriage could not be. Jean did marry a French woman and have more children, but we have never ceased being friends.

Tragically, Richard had died before we could live at Uppark together. When my father-in-law died in 1964, I had a choice once again. The choice was to sell everything and leave Uppark – I would be rich and free for other interests – or to scratch along and continue the history of the family and the family home. Without hesitation I did the latter as I felt sure this is what Richard would have wanted. So leaving my mother-in-law, Mad Meg, as she was known, to live in the house at Uppark, I moved from Bransbury with the children and into what had been a harness room in the stables. This and the attic were converted to living quarters. My recollections of inspired Italian architecture were invaluable. The builders could not see how a staircase could be incorporated into the building until I described to them how in Italy I had seen a spiral staircase winding up the trunk of a tree to the first floor. I designed a similar one and it was a success, leading from the old harness room into the attic – my daughter Harriet and family now enjoy living there.

The Uppark estate was a challenge too. I consulted my accountant, who rather cheekily asked me what I intended doing as I certainly wouldn't be able to run Uppark – a toreador waving a red rag at a bull – I, who had grown up farming, was challenged and pushed again to retort, 'On the contrary, Mr Bullen, I am going to run Uppark and if you feel it is too much for you I shall make other arrangements.' Then with wobbly legs all the way home, my course had been set. With three children at different schools it seemed right to make their permanent home at Uppark and also to have a house in London for those at day school.

My feelings at that time were difficult to sort out – I knew Uppark was right, but my mother-in-law was now at Uppark and was making life unbearable. I encouraged the girls to go over and see her in the house and she filled them with conflicting ideas about me. One day Harriet said, 'Mum, what does Greg [they called her] mean about class? Some of us are not the same as they are?' I had to try and avoid conflict and criticism but it was hard. I minded stupid things like her Spanish butler washing her car in the stable yard outside my only window. Her other grandchildren didn't dare call in to see me. The more I became involved in healing and meditation, in London by now, the less all this mattered. One amusing time, she had Richard's godmother to stay – a very dignified and grand lady, Lady Linlithgow who had been Vicereine of India, who wished to visit us for tea. So my mother-in-law brought her over, and after a brief hour said they must leave. They were sitting on a comfortable old sofa without springs, bought from the junk shop in Petersfield. My mother-in-law had struggled halfway to her feet when Lady Linlithgow's large arm swept her back and she fell into the bottomless sofa, legs flying up over her head – upon which Lady Linlithgow said she wouldn't leave as she was enjoying herself – almost the only time I saw my mother-in-law defeated. Sophie stood up to her once, asking, 'Greg, do the public PAY to see our house?' Now my mother-in-law had been brought up in very private houses, so she much resented being so exposed anyway, but worse, one should never talk about money. This was considered vulgar, so she winced and said yes, that was right, but failed to divert the conversation and an undaunted Sophie asked, 'But Greg, HOW MUCH do they pay?' She flinched.

At about this time, the co-trustees of Richard's trust bought me a small house in London. This was the greatest joy. It meant a weekend base for Harriet who was a weekly boarder at a Steiner school, and a halfway house for the others until longer spells at Upplark were possible. It also meant I was able to enjoy life and friends again, and pursue interesting activities. My healing gift came to light in a more active form, too.

During the early 1960s in London, I was taken to a rehearsal of the Royal Choral Society by a friend who introduced me to Sir Malcolm Sargent – here face to face was the man of my dreams, since I first at sixteen saw him conduct a concert in Leicester. He invited me to go to rehearsals again and our friendship grew. We dined at his table at the Savoy, we were very close and the girls adored him too. Malcolm introduced me to the world of music and musicians, a time I treasure. A most

Sir Malcolm Sargent with Harriet, Sophie and Emma

awesome experience was to drive away with him in the car from the artists' entrance after a Prom; the sudden rush of the crowd, feeling completely at their mercy and being crushed under their weight in the car. We just drove round a block or two, as he actually lived opposite the Albert Hall, but this had to remain a secret! It was magic for me to be able to go to any of his concerts and to sit in his box and be really spoilt. There were always wonderful dinner parties afterwards and he entertained many artists, ambassadors and dignitaries from the countries he had visited.

The fun during the Prom season was to know what went on behind the scenes as well as out front. Malcolm was always so kind and reassuring to young musicians, many of them performing for the first time. I remember Jacqueline du Pré being very agitated, and he was so gentle, calm and kind that she stopped throwing herself about and became quiet. But I always felt she was physically out of control, and I often thought she might fall off her chair. I wondered, did she perhaps in fact have the first signs of the disease even then? But what a privilege to have heard her incredible music making. On one occasion, John Ogden, the famous pianist, in a great state of agitation had somehow mislaid his black tie. Disaster faced him, then a bow tie on elastic fixed with a safety pin saved the day. Such seemingly small things mattered so much to keyed-up, young performers and Malcolm must have given them a feeling of such confidence with his compassion, and they went on and performed brilliantly.

On one occasion he was taking an important visitor, head of Australian broadcasting, Charles Moses, to dinner at the Savoy, where he was to be awarded an important Australian decoration. As I stepped from the car – doorman lined up – my shoe flew off and to my horror preceded me – the doorman was either too shocked or too slow to move. Should I step in a muddy road in stockings or what? In a flash this huge Australian pushed past me and leapt after the shoe, presenting it back to me with a flourish and said, 'Dear lady, I wish it could be filled with champagne.'

Once Malcolm came to stay in the stable flat at Uppark, and was very happy to have his breakfast on a tin tray and to play with the children, whom he loved. His own beloved daughter had died aged twelve, and he never really accepted this and lavished his love for her on other children. He had that great gift of being able to communicate at their level. We were all sitting at a concert once and at the front of the box during a pause in a violin concerto, twelve-year-old Harriet asked, 'S' Malcolm, do you think I will be able to play on the stage like that one day?' And he very seriously considered her question and said, 'Well darling, it might be possible but it would mean hours, days, weeks and years of practising which I don't think you would like.' And though he did not deter her ambition, it did give Harriet a happier perspective.

Malcolm always had a budgie called Hughie (more than one I think) which he would let out in the sitting-room as soon as he returned home, and it would sit on his shoulder, nibbling his ear, or on his hand as he played the piano. He was a person who really liked company. On some Sundays when Malcolm spent the day with us in London, just playing with the children or sitting in my garden at Argyll Road, I used to be rather fussed about his food. He ate very little, and I didn't have a very grand cook, but his favourite thing was stew. I said to him, 'But stew? What a funny thing to like best,' and he said, 'Well, you see, I'm always eating at grand dinner parties, and having them, and in restaurants, and no-one can ever make stew.' So that was easy, and we always had stew.

When at one time he had been very ill I went to see him and he needed something very easy to entertain him. Someone had been talking about Beatrix Potter. Malcolm did not grow up in the sort of household where you were read to at bedtime, though almost all of his friends had been brought up this way, so I solemnly read through the Beatrix Potter books – we had a lot of laughter and smiles, and I think one of his favourites was Mrs Tiggywinkle, it was such fun, recapturing the enchantment of Beatrix Potter, no matter to whom.

I was asked on one of his visits to Uppark to take him over to the house to see my mother-in-law after dinner. She appeared on the portico and greeted us dressed as for pantomime – long silvery evening dress, satin shoes, diamanté buckles and long feather boa. He had a wonderful sense of humour but also impeccable Victorian good manners – the visit was quite brief.

My mother-in-law was very keen on dressing up – I had some friends staying to shoot and we were all bidden to the big house for dinner. She had trained her Spanish butler to bow to her. As he was almost square in stature, he presented a wonderful figure as he announced dinner – you had the feeling he might topple right over. In the dining room, what should we see but the two girls from the village waiting and dressed up in Austrian dirndls, old fashioned footmen's waistcoats – black and yellow stripes, silver buttons bearing Sir Harry's crest, a stag with a feather in its mouth – and white gloves. How we managed to get through dinner with reasonably straight faces I don't know.

With three children at day school I had a bit of time and space in life in London. One Sunday coming out of church, I noticed an old man in a wheelchair sitting in the porch, alone. He seemed to be waiting but the church was empty – no-one came. The following Sunday I saw the same thing and was compelled to speak to him. He was glad of an offer to push him home – he lived like I did at the top of Camden Hill and he was a large man, I hadn't realised what I'd taken on – however I managed to deliver him to his very shabby home. He was very knowledgeable about opera and music and a most interesting person who had fallen on hard times. The surroundings were very grubby and I had to curb my enthusiasm to help when offered a bun from an old paper bag – and he made me think deeply about people like him. This was when I joined the WVS to do meals on wheels, a brilliant service and superbly organised. Three mornings a week a driver picked me up and we were allotted a very poor area including Rillington Place where there had recently been a spate of notorious murders. I was only allowed ten minutes for each delivery, and I came to see how wise this was as I could very easily have become deeply involved in people's troubles, both emotionally and materially, and this was not my work. The ten minutes were so precious to the recipients. It was not the food people wanted, it was the human contact, compassion, a sounding board for their woes, communication and above all, touch.

Enormous barriers could be broken down by just a hand on the shoulder, or a pat on the knee. It often seemed to open the floodgates of despair, loneliness and psychological starvation. They were mostly uneducated people, each one of value – the Irishman who spent all his money on the horses, we talked racing and always had a laugh. He was a happy man and he had nothing – one room, one huge chair from a skip, and the room knee-deep in newspapers which he said were much warmer than blankets and were easier to change.

There was a miserable old crone full of woe because she said she couldn't see anything in life – her basement room was very dark, the atmosphere grim. I talked to her about light, then rubbed a hole in a blackened pane of glass and told her to keep looking through it at the light. The next time I went she was better and said, 'I see what you mean about light.' The room was just as dark, but she had begun to see with her inner eye and her thoughts were of less material things. It is a rewarding moment when someone says, 'I see,' in understanding.

These months of meals on wheels led me to commit myself to healing through laying on hands – essentially in my own house, where I could be a free spirit and invite whoever I wished.

Thinking deeply about how vital light is to people, sometimes it seemed almost more than food, I felt inspired to go to Greece. I toured some of the islands and mainland sites with a Greek guide who had been steeped all her life in myths and tales of Gods and Heroes – the best teacher I could have had. On arrival in Greece, by the sea I exclaimed out loud, 'Now I see what crystal clear means.' I was amazed not only by the almost blinding light but the clarity of everything; the colours, the sights, sounds and smells and above all the sparkling crystal sea.

The siting of magnificent temples and other buildings was awesome in their perfection. They had been built in harmony with nature and sacred architecture, each measurement with an esoteric meaning. In all these places stories of The Gods were easily believed – the oracles at Delphi easily possible – there where it is written over an entrance 'Man know thyself and thou shalt know the Universe'. These words stuck fast. Almost the most memorable visit was to the island of Patmos. Riding up a rough, steep and rocky path to the monastery on a donkey seemed like a pilgrimage. We participated in a service with monks in long black robes, black round hats, black beards and with very beady black eyes (there were rarely visitors in those days). I was completely carried away by the Gregorian chant in such beautiful deep voices in that particular place. We were shown the cave where St John had his Revelations and were shown a book of finest pale mauve vellum on which these were written. There were more places of great beauty for other reasons. Epidaurus with the theatre whose sound could be heard a great distance from its very centre to the furthest seats – seats incidently built to very specific numbers and placing.

I thought much more about light and sound, and the effects of buildings with exact measurements in the right places. The pure physical beauty which Greeks worshipped showed in statues of perfect bodies made me realize how much all these things contributed to healing. This was the first of many travels to further my quest for knowledge – one thing leading to another.

While I was living in the stable flat in 1962, I went to visit my father in Rhodesia and did not like it. I had looked forward to the visit, but when I stepped off the plane I was shocked – the atmosphere was not hot, dry and comfortable like Spain. It was hot, damp and very heavy. I smelt blood. However, I entered into the spirit of the visit, saw the Victoria Falls and men building on the Kariba Dam, which was situated in a valley on land that was sacred to Africans, and a tribal place. As the native people predicted, there was trouble there – we cannot go against nature. Here, now in year 2001 (at the time of writing), despite all our modern technology, no-one can do anything to stop the winds and floods causing devastation, nor the breakdown of stock exchange computers and much else. We would do well to listen – perhaps in spite of financial loss – to warnings based on the ancient teachings of people who live close to nature. The Kariba Dam burst, drowning hundreds of men. It was rebuilt but it has not fulfilled the original hopes for it, and I would not be surprised if it does not last.

I watched my brother-in-law's African employees harvesting tobacco, in rhythm but silent. I asked him whether they did not sing while working. He thought a while, and said, 'Well yes, I suppose they used to when I was young, but they don't any more.' The way the working men were treated seemed quite out of tune. Later of course, their feelings were manifested in riots. I went on to stay in South Africa with a much loved uncle in Natal. He painted, and was a magician with birds and wild animals. He kept a pet leopard cub, and he would sit with it in his garden, saying, 'Keep still, I'll show you a humming bird.' Within minutes, one would be on the garden seat or on his shoulder; the same with a lyre bird, and all kinds of brightly coloured birds. He was so good to his servants too, unlike what I had seen in Rhodesia.

On my flight back, I was able to do as I had hoped, and made a break, getting off in Khartoum. I had briefed myself with an Egyptologist at the British Museum beforehand in case I could see Egypt. Khartoum in the middle of night was grim. There was to be a domestic flight in five hours time at 6 a.m., and looking around, I felt I couldn't stay one hour.

Egypt

I saw the BA pilots disappearing, so I ran after them and asked them how I could get to Cairo. They were splendid and within half an hour I was on my way in a small Egyptian plane to Cairo – things did not go quite as planned though. I'd heard of Shepheard's Hotel (equivalent to the Ritz in London) so made for that. There, the hall poster told me traveller's cheques were not valid in Egypt. This was just at the time of the Nasser coup. Anyway, I went to bed and after a good breakfast got sorted out. Anyone to whom I had an introduction had disappeared – it was a very dangerous climate. A willing black market for money transpired and a guide who had been recommended was produced. He was a nephew of the guide who had been with Howard Carter and Lord Carnarvon when they discovered Tutankhamen's tomb. I had time in Cairo to see this marvellous tomb and relics in the museum. Seeing the sun rise on the Nile was utterly beautiful. I visited the pyramids and the Sphinx. My visit to the Great Pyramid at Giza was overwhelming, and I experienced a peculiar kind of fear. While I was in the shaft going up small steps into the king's chamber, I suddenly felt detached from the world, claustrophobic yet in space at alternate moments, both vulnerable and suffocating. There I was, in a shaft in the Pyramid, with a stranger whom I had been handed over to at the entrance with my pearls around my neck and all my valuables in my handbag. Not a soul to be heard, and no-one would have any idea where I was. Since then, I recognise like all my travels chosen intuitively, how essential to my learning this particular trip was.

I knew later that ancient wisdom came from Hermes to the Egyptians, and the pharaohs who were initiated into this knowledge passed it on and so through history. I visited vast temples, nearly fainting at El-Karnak (Hermonthis), just around the corner I found a statue of the cat god, Bast. I thought there must be a connection in a past life somewhere! I hated cats.

I flew down to Luxor to see the marvels there. Visiting the tombs in the Valley of the Kings, I went down these wonderful painted shafts leading deep underground, to the tombs all illustrated with hieroglyphics and information; seemingly they had been painted without direct natural light. It was reflected by mirrors all the way down.

Returning to Uppark was also like emerging from a rather curious underground passage – fascinating, mysterious and rather sinister under the weight of so much history.

Two years later my father died and I made my second visit to Rhodesia. I flew with a plane-load of journalists, returning residents and others all in a fuss as the Unilateral Declaration of Independence was about to be declared. I re-booked my passage home every day for fear I would be stuck there. Things were very uneasy. My father was cremated in a service the like of which I had not seen before, and of course the sudden horror of seeing this beloved person's coffin disappear into a hole in the wall proved too much for me and I dissolved. My married sister, Susan, living over there, put me together again. I was glad to be with her and her family, but I was glad to be going home, away from the uneasy atmosphere which has since proved a correct premonition, alas, so back to Uppark and London life.

CHAPTER SIX

Argyll Road

Argyll Road – John Tooley – Covent Garden Opera House – Maria Callas – Russian Ballet – Ian and Susan Hunter – Menuhins – Bruce MacManaway – Bernie – Healing and Argyll Road – John Petty – Donald Reeves – St Roc Trust

AFTER SOME YEARS IN LONDON, I moved to a larger house in Argyll Road, Kensington. This was the peak of my life, steering my daughters through school and their parties in their teens, setting up my healing clinic which involved a lot of learning, and there was spiritual growth and a good social life. I entertained musicians, ambassadors, artists, dancers and many others.

The house was a wonderful new space for my daughters to grow up in – Harriet left school to train as a Cordon Bleu chef, and shared the basement as her own flat with friends. She was also having a low-key debutante season. I gave a dance for her and she went to parties, but being quite shy she found it hard, I think. I found other mothers more sophisticated than me and quite pushy, but Harriet had good friends. I saw off many young men, who are now prosperous in high up places and society, as unsuitable boyfriends! They all seem to have forgiven me, even those who didn't get through the net.

Though in her own flat, this was also Harriet's family home, and if she was unwell or isolated, she had only to unlock the door and come upstairs. I think being in the parental home made it easier to deal with uncircumspect parties! If only many other parents could find how this helps; not to interfere, but just to be there, if and when needed. This was indeed a beautiful house, made for parties and I had many. The most enjoyable up to sixteen people, buffets with best silver, and lots of moving about as I knew how awful it was to get stuck with someone and become bored. I once got stuck at an embassy party with an Egyptian ambassador who proceeded to tell me the history of Egypt – and it's a long one – it took all evening and no-one saved me! If he had talked about the ancient Egyptian mysteries, temple myths and Pyramids, I would have enjoyed it, but I learnt all this much later.

One friend, John Tooley, manager of Covent Garden Opera House, spoilt me with visits to the opera over the years, and to now legendary concerts. The experience of the ballets and concerts took me away from this world and all my difficulties into a state of bliss. I was at first rather shattered to share worries behind the scenes when in Wagner's *Ring* Siegfried sprained his Achilles tendon and could not jump off a rock – somehow he lost his glamour. The same when a diva, after a superb performance, with the curtain falling began bargaining for higher pay; when a world famous artist seemed worried only about his wife's infidelity, and on and on. John had to shoulder much more than artistic matters!

Parties at Argyll Road, London

Listening to music is balm for the soul, and this was the subject of a conversation with violinists David and Igor Oistrakh, just allowed through the Iron Curtain, over dinner at the Savoy after their concert. Though their English wasn't good, they conveyed that to them music was cosmic and universal to those who can really hear it. In the hermetic teachings, music was absolutely essential in order to understand all else – harmony and numbers are the building blocks of the universe.

On another occasion I met Maria Callas after one of her memorable performances of *Tosca* at Covent Garden. She was very down to earth – charming and with the great gift of being interested in others. She asked how many children I had and then plucked a rose for each of them, now dried and cherished by the girls. When the Russian ballet, the Bolshoi, first emerged from behind the Iron Curtain, I invited them for dinner at Argyll Road after the ballet. Seeing the Russians dance was a really breathtaking experience – pure magic – they seemed to dance with their souls, and in their private lives too. Language seemed less important to them and they met one on a meaningful level. They really practised empathy in their whole way of being. Natalia Dudinskaya and Sergiev Constantin had brought the company over and six of them came to dinner, which lasted until dawn. They had never been in a private home

Parties at Uppark

in the west, and non-communist life amazed them. They wanted to examine the kitchen, my clothes, children's rooms, presumably everything which they had been denied. The second time they came over, they visited again. One of their company was suffering a migraine and was on very bad form, so was taken home early. The following day, newspaper headlines: one of Russia's finest ballerinas had defected to the west – our guest. A few years later, the ballet came with a different company, as Dudinskaya and Constantin had been sacked and deprived of their house. This time the party asked to bring an interpreter, and when asked why (we had got along fine without before), it seemed more than likely to us that he was, in fact, from the KGB. He was clearly worried when, after dinner, age groups split up, with the older people in the drawing room, answering questions on subjects ranging from how many pairs of shoes we had to where we bought meat, the younger ones going to the next room where a most attractive young dancer played folk songs on a guitar. This dancer was very homesick but they had fun. However a few days later he absconded. This was the famous dancer Mikhail Baryshnikov. I went to see him backstage at Covent Garden some while later after he had achieved his ambition – he had danced the lead in *Romeo and Juliet* but his feet were bleeding. Triumphant he was but in subsequent years damaged. He went on to form his own company in the USA – but what a dancer – like all Russians, music and dance in their very soul. They cannot be taught, only trained – if only all peoples had this quality and could manifest it the world would change. What did my children learn at school? Russian children all learn philosophy – ours alas do not – on and on we talked until dawn. Russians have no idea of time anyway. I was touched when a parcel arrived from Russia later – this was a live recording of the famous pianist Richter playing Scriabin, which I later used when making a video – a great thank-you.

I became a friend of Ian and Susan Hunter who were most kind to me. Ian launched and managed many music festivals, the Bath Festival, London, Edinburgh, Windsor and others. But the most interesting introduction to me was to the Menuhins. Ian was Yehudi's impresario and often invited me to meet him and have dinner after a concert. Yehudi was almost not of this world – he emanated benificence – his smile seemed to create harmony wherever it shone. He had such enchanting, almost fairy-tale visions which often were not at all practical or possible. But whenever I met him he had a new idea for the betterment of the world. Of course, his music did this all the time. I could hardly believe that he was a musician who had played the violin, aged nine, for Elgar, and my most precious memories are of concerts listening to Yehudi playing. His wife Diana was great fun and a good raconteur – her stories of their travels and experiences always made good listening. They once came back with me to Uppark after a concert in Chichester to have dinner with my mother-in-law. We laughed afterwards as they had pictured dinner in a hall with a blazing log fire and all the trappings, and all we got was a miserable dinner in freezing cold in a room with the one-bar electric fire!

Diana and I rushed upstairs to put on our woolly tights, but Yehudi probably didn't notice; he always seemed to rise above such situations, but we did leave very soon afterwards. I was driving back to London, and Yehudi, in his typically thoughtful way, insisted as the roads were icy that his chauffeur kept my car in view all the way to be sure I arrived safely. The most fun of the festivals was Bath – small, intimate and we all had supper in a charming little restaurant near the concert hall. One year the Russian Symphony Orchestra arrived with great flourish, a triumph from behind the Iron Curtain – Yehudi's playing with them was so beautiful it seemed unearthly – but the merriment afterwards grounded us all. Even after death, Yehudi's glorious playing seems to go on in the ether and in all the goodness of works that he left. His memorial service at Westminster Abbey was a truly memorable occasion. It was a gathering of all who had loved him, all denominations, all countries, all races of people, and of so many others whose lives he had touched. He certainly did all he could in his life to create a harmonious whole.

It was while I was in Argyll Road that healing began as a total commitment. I went to a healing conference where I met the healer I had been to years before, Bruce MacManaway. He said, 'I have been waiting for this moment for years. Now you will begin to dowse and heal.' He had made a successful TV programme, and was flooded with requests for healing, so I suggested we work in my large house.

The house became overwhelmed with a huge mixture of people – not always pleasant – but always a powerful feeling of healing pervaded. Bruce had a young man called Bernie who had been training with him, and with whom I instantly clicked, feeling *déjà vu*. Bernie was very small but he had a huge shock of black afro-frizz hair of which he was very proud, and of course this made him look at least a foot taller!

Bernie was such a character – half my age, from the outskirts of Liverpool from a very modest background – no family and lots of common sense. He was a powerful healer, indeed, and best of all with the most wonderful sense of humour. We sat down on our first day and he said, 'You know, Jean, we are committing ourselves to a path which once we are on we can never leave,' and he was right. We worked so closely together we didn't need to speak, and at times when things were unpleasant or rough we'd laugh, and I laughed with Bernie more than with anyone else I've ever known. One day we had Barbara Cartland in a pink velvet dress. Bernie was putting his healing hands on her back when I noticed he was leaving marks like dinner plates on her dress, so tactfully, I tried to convey this and words came out wrong. She realised her dress was suffering and with a quick zip it fell to her feet and there she stood in a satin and lace petticoat. Bernie, who had never seen anything like this before, was astounded. After a successful healing session, she left and we doubled up laughing at what could have been a dress disaster. On many occasions being near to tears turned to laughter as we shared experiences, which made life much more enjoyable. When Bernie first came to work with me his appearance was unorthodox, with rings and chains and open sandals and the kit, but after some years Bernie changed like we all do because of what was happening and the people he was with, and perhaps because of Hardy Amies the famous couturier. Hardy was amused by Bernie and so were some of his friends who were recommended for healing too, and Bernie was invited to stay in some very grand houses. I warned him of one or two traps he might fall into because I knew it wasn't really Bernie's background and I felt it might take him a little while to recover from the shock and really feel at home in this enviroment. I didn't want him to get hurt, but everyone always adored him, particularly for the best sense of humour, so things always ended with gales of laughter. So Bernie set off on his first visit, to be met at the station by a chauffeur. When he arrived the butler asked for his luggage. He only had a paper bag containing pyjamas and a toothbrush; on his next visit he was asked for his cases so his clothes could be ironed for him, which meanwhile he had acquired. We laughed about him cutting out Marks & Spencer labels to look as if the clothes came from somewhere much grander. But Bernie was a tremendous success, and as time went on his clothes got smarter and his confidence was enormous. Some of our patients would request private healing at their home, which I certainly wasn't prepared to do, but Bernie was and found himself invited to stay in the grandest homes. After we had worked together for years he eventually went off to New York to work on his own merits, and his wonderful references stood him in good stead. He became an interior decorator and continues to be a powerful healer, but sadly just a few years ago we lost contact. Bernie has achieved a large part of his vision.

After some time the atmosphere didn't seem quite right and my inner voice said: watch out! I had to change the plan and suggested Bruce went elsewhere. This was hard to do as he had set me on a path of healing others, but we must trust our intuition and I did.

Bernie chose to work with me, and we suffered a sort of punishment for some months. At a workshop Bruce had given, I met a young clergyman, John Petty, who was to become not only a great healer, but at that time my saviour from very unpleasant happenings. Bernie and I felt we were being demolished by inexplicable things – horrible telephone calls, strange psychic messages to people working for me, and recorded telephone messages of where I would be going and what I'd be doing when only I knew – very sinister. After months of such events, John, by the power of prayer, overcame these things. His holiness cleared the air. Bernie and I had a full and busy clinic. The experiences with Bruce were now water under the bridge, and there were many more bridges ahead but not as dangerous. Laughter is really a great healer and we used to laugh when work was done, and during work too. The Russians say there is just one string linking chaos to the universe and that string is laughter. People would often seek help and healing in a tense and worried state. If one can get them to laugh, it breaks the tension and helps them heal on all levels. Once into this stream of consciousness, for that's what healing is like, I began to meet interesting people who were on a different wavelength with different motives in life – a motive of compassion – healers attract healers like a magnet. Healing energy after all is magnetic. One day, John Petty brought along another clergyman, Donald Reeves. He was a dynamic person and a wonderful preacher and an organist of merit. This was the beginning of a long friendship and partnership between the three of us. Realising that healing was almost spoken of in whispers, I formed a registered charity trust with some money I had been left by my uncle in South Africa.

John and Donald became trustees of this St Roc Healing Trust, and all through these many years and vicissitudes they have staunchly stood by me, the best healers I could have journeyed with. The St Roc Healing Trust became an extension of my home, and I was free to co-ordinate with all religions, orthodox and unorthodox medicines and many holistic practitioners and doctors. During these years, I was also on a pilgrimage myself. A healer has to heal him or herself – life being the greatest teacher.

We must learn to grow from the 'good' and 'bad' things which happen to us, as well as the joy in life. All things seem later to have happened for some good reason.

Healing Hands

CHAPTER SEVEN

Dowsing and the St Roc Trust

Dowsing – Bach Flower Remedies – St Roc Trust – Medical and Scientific Network – Vichy

During my nursing years, I had found I could help patients very much by literally just holding their hands. I later found I could help my husband's asthma attacks by laying my hands on him. I was taught by Bruce how to use a pendulum instead of a divining rod to show a positive or negative answer. Most people find a pendulum suspended on a loose thread will swing clockwise or vice versa if they ask it to show positive or negative. I find that my pendulum swings back and forth for positive and side to side for negative.

This, combined with the power through my hands, has brought much

St Roc Trust, Healing Service

healing to ill people. Experience taught me to diagnose both disease and problems, since most disease is psychosomatic. That is not to say the illness isn't real, but that it is caused by a disharmony in the emotions. So I would first observe how I felt, what my intuition was telling me, then check my results using the pendulum. It has become increasingly clear that most illness is caused by inner disease and tension. In many instances a patient comes with outward manifestations of sickness such as back trouble, neck, leg or shoulder pains, migraine, etc. I run my hands down the spine, checking with my pendulum for places where the spine may be out of alignment. Then I treat this, possibly with some gentle laying on of hands. This usually relieves the pressure which has been causing the pain on the nerves, and releases muscular tension in the area. From there, I work on until I feel I reach the cause of the patient's trouble. This may take several sessions. Each time I use my pendulum, I check its movements for positive and negative. Occasionally the pendulum won't answer at all, in which case I do nothing, or it might swing wildly all over the place. This means great disturbance, but I always completely trust my pendulum. Sometimes healing takes the form of words spoken. In this area, healing directs the cosmic energies to enable the patient to find their centre; a centre from which they can draw strength and love. Personally, my centre is based on Christianity; from this source I know all cosmic energies can be drawn. A meditation is very helpful too. I give it as an exercise and it is something positive the patient can take home with them and do for themselves as self-help is necessary for healing to occur.

I also use my pendulum to choose Bach Flower Remedies – Doctor Bach found healing formulas in flower essences and there are now many more known. By questioning the pendulum I arrive at the remedy most helpful to a particular patient, and also the correct dose. There are now scientists using biofeedback to measure vibratory rates, revealing where best a healer can lay their hands. This is not always where the pain is. I find I can determine the same things, using a pendulum with less disturbance to the patient. I can only say I thank God daily for allowing me to be a channel for healing.

I was faced with my first patient to treat on my own – a grief-stricken, angry young woman who sat down and declared, 'You won't be able to help me or to understand. I'm thirty-six, have three small children and my husband has died suddenly, leaving me stranded.' I was listening to a replica of my own experiences, and when I told her this, a look of first incredulity, then of sad relief came over her face. I put my hands on her shoulders and from then on something happened and healing began for both of us, because I suddenly was able to say to myself, NOW I see why this happened to me, so that I can help other people. The more one is aware of a deeper reason, the more healing can take place.

It was now that I had my first out-of-body experience – I had heard of this sort of thing happening, so I was less frightened than I could have been. As I put my hands on the young woman, I suddenly felt as though I was floating up to the ceiling. I was looking down on the scene and the whole room and as I realised I had left my body, my reaction was to think I mustn't let go of the earth or I shall not get back – I must stay here – I returned to my body that instant. It could only have been seconds – I was out of time, but later I was glad to have experienced this – I understood some things which later happened a lot better. In times of terrible trauma and grief, the same experience happened to me again and perhaps made what was taking place less awful by being more detached.

When travelling in Spain I had been searching for a name for our trust, and in every small church there was the patron saint of healers, Saint Roc, or Roche. Saint Roche was born in 1337 and lived in France. It was while he was on his way to Rome, where his uncle was Pope, that he discovered he had the gift of healing, and healed many Europeans suffering from the plague. His statue is often seen wearing a pilgrim's cloak hung with scallop shells and with a dog at his side. St Roc healed all his life, and is buried in the Middle East.

Establishing the St Roc Healing Trust, while dealing with a million other difficulties in life, John and Donald were towers of strength to me, giving advice and help freely. They have also travelled a long way in their own thinking. John is now Provost of Coventry Cathedral and Donald is Rector of St James' Church, Piccadilly in the heart of London.

It was in my house that the first meeting took place of the Medical and Scientific Network. I met the scientist Sir Kelvin Spencer, who had the idea of forming an association for doctors and healers to meet. At that time no respectable doctor dared mention the word healer, so the doctors here had only Christian names – no address and no telephone number. They met in my house with healers until things got going. The Medical and Scientific Network is now a very flourishing concern. Several of these brave doctors came back into my life many years later when I had a healing clinic and doctors dared to declare their work with the so-called unorthodox.

Then I became very tired, and went to various doctors for help. Homeopathy did not help, orthodox specialists seemed unable to cure my problem which was a form of hepatitis, then not well-known. I knew about many watering places for cures on the Continent, of course, so I went to Vichy in France. Vichy was a spa resort, but very much more sophisticated than Mont d'Or where Richard and I had been. Years had gone by and I think many more people attended these places and more facilities had been opened up. Like Mont d'Or Vichy had many springs coming from volcanic rock, each with different mineral content. I lay in baths, was sprayed, massaged, lay in the mud at Vichy's water pools, and drank and drank. The water was so strong I had to do all this under the supervision of a doctor. The head doctor in Vichy was also a marvellous dietician – only a French doctor could manage to keep someone well and happy while doing this appallingly tough cure, at the same time as eating good food and drinking good wine. His joke was that I could drink wine as long as it was château-bottled. This was all right in France, but the look of horror when I returned to London and told my friends ... anyway the cure did me a lot of good.

I happened to know the manager of the largest hotel in the area, and was from time to time invited to a party or dinner there. At one of these, in my frivolous way, I had mentioned that I had a Guernsey herd in England which was very large and well-known, and the head of the Charolais Society was produced some time later to meet me. Without really being interested, and not meaning to, I found myself swept into a sort of agricultural, social whirl and an enormous lunch was given in my honour as the owner of the Uppark herd! The food was a disaster as I had to be very careful about what I ate, and the conversation was interesting but absolutely entirely about these huge white Charolais cattle. We then spent the rest of the very hot day going around enormous farms and artificial insemination centres, looking at large Charolais, middle sized Charolais, small Charolais and Charolais of every sort and kind. At the end of the day I was given the most magnificent certificate to say I was an honorary member of the Charolais Society, and that was enough.

After three weeks there I returned and though I felt most dreadfully tired it certainly made the most enormous difference to my hepatitis, and I was cured. My doctor at Vichy, before I left, gave me several warnings, once saying, 'Madame, I am about to deal you a death blow because I know how you enjoy life, but you may never touch champagne again or it will kill you.' He had a great sense of humour, and he did laugh, but he meant what he said, and he added, 'I can assure you I know what I am saying because I had hepatitis and married Mademoiselle Roederer, so I understand how awful it will be.' The Roederers were large producers of champagne. I got very much better through the years, and I did the cure a second year. Now in my old age I enjoy the occasional glass of champagne, but certainly I saw the red light.

Back in circulation once more and feeling better after the cure, I began healing again. I felt a need for more knowledge, more learning. It was hard to mix the people I entertained in Argyll Road and many did not want to hear about healing and what they called, in their ignorance or fear, these occult things. The Church was very fearful, and I had many abusive calls and letters from clergymen. This of course changed completely through the years. I seemed always to be a pioneer. I was able to attend many healing workshops and conferences, always seeking more.

CHAPTER EIGHT

Wrekin Trust

Sir George Trevelyan – Wrekin Trust – Frédéric Lionel – Dr Alec Forbes – Harry Edwards – Dr John Lester

THEN I MET SIR GEORGE TREVELYAN again, a great man of immense learning and in touch with higher vibrations, and with esoteric knowledge. He realised the need for adult spiritual learning and he founded the Wrekin Trust. Sir George came from a long line of Trevelyans, an aristocratic family of academics who had lived from around the eleventh century in their ancestral home Wallington in Northumberland. He was one of a family of six, and was not satisfied, but was a seeker in life. He went to a lecture about compost, and said compost started him off on a path of awakening which he never left. The thought of compost and constant recycling back into the earth put him on to the work of Rudolf Steiner and anthroposophy (the study of the Mind of Man), theosophy and philosophy. He pursued many avenues and studied, and became head tutor in a very large house called Attingham, which was set up as a college for the further education of adults after the war. Here he found a kind of special after-war enthusiasm which was leading to a second renaissance of thought. There were many young people too who were not satisfied with the way they were living, and these were to become the advanced souls who would lead the so-called New Age movement with Sir George. At Attingham, he held weekends which he discovered were very popular if they were of a spiritual nature. Sir George was disinherited from his family and his beautiful ancestral home because of his unorthodox ways. His way was to enable seekers to spend weekends in attractive large houses in order to hear speakers from different religions, cults, beliefs and professions. There were discussions which otherwise could not easily happen among open-minded people with a common thirst for spiritual wisdom. Sir George was a brilliant orator and used the English language in the best way. He had huge courage as at that time, what he was doing in an academic form, was what Flower Power people and the Beatles were doing in other ways – breaking away from the conditioned, conventional mould. The courses were too free-thinking for Attingham, and eventually he left there to do something even more progressive in setting up the Wrekin Trust. He had a holistic vision, and his courses would inspire an alternative way of life, to help people become stewards of the planet, not exploiters. He called for recognition among people that we should recognise the intelligence of the earth. Sir George lived to a great age and the last impression I have of him is on a video made not very long before he died and he recited a poem which begins:

> Man, tread softly on the Earth
> What looks likes dust
> Is also stuff of which galaxies are made.

Later at one of the many conferences held by Sir George, he introduced a Frenchman called Frédéric Lionel.

Frédéric Lionel was born in 1908, and trained as a scientist. During the war, he joined the French Underground and was dropped behind enemy lines. At a time of desperate danger he stayed with a Spaniard named Garcia. An alchemist and truly enlightened master, Garcia enabled Frédéric to awaken to a different vision and to reach a higher state of consciousness.

Frédéric Lionel

A philosopher, sage and writer, he was the most inspiring guide for all those concerned with profound inner changes taking place in our society. Frédéric called himself an alchemist, and as soon as I heard him it was like being a wobbly nail hammered home by a strong blow! I knew his words meant a great deal to me, and even though I didn't fully understand them, something bigger and more powerful went home. I knew this was something I wanted to hear more of – Frédéric struck a chord with each word. Even when twenty-five years later I listen to his words I hear something more I need to know. I gathered a small group of like-minded people and organised for him to come from his Paris home to spend weekends with us. He didn't want to be called a guru or teacher – he was a transmitter of knowledge from a higher source. I listened to him both abroad and in England for years and he gave me a new vision of life.

Sir George often quoted Christopher Fry's *Sleep of Prisoners*:

> Thank God our time is now when wrong
> Comes up to face us everywhere
> Never to leave us till we take
> The longest stride of Soul man ever took
> Affairs are now soul size
> The enterprise is exploration into God
> Wake up

When I met Christopher Fry years later, I was able to tell him how often I had used his words to help people wake up. This was what people had to do – and do it now. Sir George was showing the ways in which one could do this. Weekend conferences helped many to expand their awareness and reach other dimensions, and his courses rapidly developed, such was the need, as well as courses in complementary therapies which were starting to gain recognition as the limitations of conventional medicine were felt. All this opened up a new vision of wholeness – a freedom of thought into other areas which the frightened would avoid, preferring to remain encased in the familiar.

When I went to the first Wrekin Trust weekend conference on healing, someone came up whom I recognised: a very tall doctor named Alec Forbes. It was quite extraordinary – during the war when I was training at the Radcliffe, Alec had been a junior house doctor and we became friends – I remember being very flattered when this very serious Scots doctor asked me out to dinner. Apart from his great appreciation for good wine, I didn't remember anything, so it was a surprise to find him at a Wrekin Trust healing conference. He had spent many years as head physician at Plymouth General Hospital and as soon as he could, he began to study healing therapies in a very big way. Alec moved on, and very bravely set up what he called health centres in out-of-the-way villages, a pioneering effort to provide a drop-in centre with information on therapies which no other doctor would have anything to do with. He took me to a lecture he was giving at Guy's Hospital, where young doctors and nurses were so keen to hear about healing that there were people sitting outside the hall. Alec came to stay with me several times in London with the idea of setting up a clinic to combine conventional and traditional medicine with doctors and therapists. We hoped to set this up in London, but as time went on it was clear that neither of us was interested in administration. There was no money to back a rather vast enterprise and then Alec decided he would rather specialise in cancer and I most definitely did not want to specialise because I wanted more of everything. At that moment he met the Pilkingtons who had financial help and he set up with them the now very well-known Bristol Cancer Help Centre. This pioneering centre had many ups and downs, but it was a very successful new effort, backed by Prince Charles, who also had courage, which sowed the seed for many other such centres in other places. Alec used to send his London patients to me at my healing centre, and we had a very interesting partnership for many years until we both moved into different areas, and Alec went out to live in New Zealand. His name certainly goes down in the history of medicine as it is becoming now, integrated, to provide health for the whole person.

A friend suggested I went to see a great healer, Harry Edwards, as I had a query. I was apprehensive about public healing and trusting my own ability. He was a great old man, very straightforward, no-nonsense and very powerful. I asked him how I would know if I was worthy of this great and precious gift. Could I and should I use it for others? He took my hands and clapped them on to a patient he was treating, saying, 'Now my dear, God has given you these hands and made you as you are – get on with it and use them as you feel.' I spent many days with Harry Edwards who encouraged me a lot. I realised the absolute necessity of complementary healing, working with doctors and other therapies. For this reason, I have always remained unattached to any specific group, and worked from my own home.

The clinic grew and grew, mostly by word of mouth. Soon, I met an interested doctor, and from then on the co-ordination of healing and orthodox medicine grew. Through the years I have been joined by several well-known doctors, each of them searching for something more, and who like me were walking their own spiritual path. Each doctor taught me a lot about his particular field, and has spent time with me, sometimes years. I also began to have patients returning who had been to me for healing and who were starting out on their own path, healing and needing to work with someone experienced. Healing touch seemed to awaken people's intuition and the healing power in their own hands. I have always been blessed in meeting the right person at the right time. I met a Harley Street doctor, John Lester, also Dean of the London College of Osteopathy. We talked about Rudolf Steiner's work (Harriet was at a Steiner school) and his philosophy which I studied for years. This led to more interests in common. This doctor eventually came to live in my house and we sometimes worked together. He found he had far more successful results when his patients had healing before or during osteopathic treatments, and this led up many other avenues, explorations of therapies and philosophies and beliefs. He was a disciple and a teacher of the work of Gurdjieff and had sat at his feet. The Work (as Gurdjieff's teachings are known) is a ferociously disciplined sect and is almost impossible to live with unless everyone participates. It eventually made our partnership impossible.

As I gained knowledge the type of patient changed. They came by word of mouth so this was organic – nothing else. To start with I had people with bad backs, sprains, stiff necks, elbows, legs and straightforward physical complaints that doctors and hospitals had failed with. Once John Lester sent me a man who had a non-stop twitching foot; he couldn't work, sleep, walk, do anything. The doctor said, 'We have tried everything and there is no alternative but an operation (to cut the tendon) or *you*!'

With one healing laying on of hands the twitch started to quieten. His wife came too and I felt she was also a healer so she joined me. This man came several times and his foot completely stopped twitching (checked with the doctor all along); he went back to work, to play football and become normal again. His wife went on to help others with her healing hands. There were hundreds of such things that happened and in practically every case I always managed to laugh with the patient. Laughter is more important than we any of us realise, it can heal wounds of body and soul.

Melissa Fairbanks came with her knee immobilised and having an operation next day. I said miracles do not happen, but they do. I heard myself telling Melissa to cherish her knee – to love it and treat it like a sick child – not to be angry and blame it for stopping an important filming dancing role she was in. She accepted this, her knee returned to normal size and the operation was cancelled. Later the surgeon remarked he would like to have operated to see how this cure could have happened!

It seemed as if during the time I was balancing family, clinic, learning, fun in life that I felt from time to time in my travels that I needed a balance of energy/thought. When I had been to a place where dowsing was involved, and where the mysterious ancient ceremonies had been carried out, some bloodthirsty – and where energies had been manipulated in an occult way (meaning that which is outside the limitation of man's thinking) that I was then drawn to the opposite. When I had been in Mexico I felt the need for something Christian and holy, when I had been in Ireland dowsing I went then to holy places in monasteries and abbeys. After many different visits to mysterious places I went to Spain to the sea and to be quite still.

At one time I went to Italy with John while I was working in a marvellous partnership with him of osteopathy and healing. He was the best travelling companion I have ever had. I usually travelled alone when one can make contract with anyone or no-one but this time we toured the beautiful sights in Umbria together. Italy is one of the best places to travel a short distance to see much. An Italian friend who came to stay suggested a tour of Umbria. Italians are so proud of their country. He knew all the small exquisite places where we should go.

John had a vast spiritual esoteric knowledge which applied to the very holy pictures we saw. We went to Assisi and saw the Giotto frescoes (since ruined) which were the first pictures I ever learnt about. To see the real thing was awesome – the aura of light round St Francis's hands as he fed the birds, and the halos (auras) around holy people's heads was stunning. We went outside Assisi to the hermitage where St Francis built a retreat – a tiny cell-like room with a window out of which he must have looked at the heavenly view. I could so easily feel how it must have felt to meditate in that little cell. It reminded me of others in other places: Scotland, Ireland, Spain. Somehow the saintliness of the artists in those very early days seemed to have got painted. The frescos of Piero della Francesca had an unearthly feel about them.

The illustrated books and manuscripts in the cathedral in Urbino had such gold and such work of lifetimes in them, the colours still much as

Sir George Trevelyan

they would have been when applied. We drove up mountains to tiny villages where probably in the church we would find a gem – in one we came across Fra Filippo Lippi's *Annunciation*, a picture I was given as a child and which I have had all my life beside my bed. There were many more wonderful places and each one seemed to add more light to my understanding. It was like travelling a path lit by candles all along the way. John being an Australian, therefore very practical and self supporting, was splendid when our hired car broke down miles from anywhere at night. He picked the engine to pieces, by which time a curious and helpful Italian had joined us, then proceeded with our new friend to put it together again with the addition of a bit of wire, and off we went. We had a lot of happy travels.

CHAPTER NINE

Patients and Pilgrimage

Types of patients – David Tansley – Lambert Mount – Pilgrimage to Santiago de Compostela, Spain

IN THE 1970S AT ARGYLL ROAD, the healing clinic was in full swing. Apart from doctors, many other interesting people came and went, one being David Tansley. David was a pioneer in many ways, not only of radionics but of spiritual knowledge too. He read the works of Alice Bailey the theosophist, and much else. He started life studying agriculture. He went on to philosophy and then to study deeply with a Zen master, and to comparative religion. As his awareness grew, he went further into all this and realised that there was more to man than meets the physical eye – he brought together sculpting and religion, and had great success in America with his sculpture and also his skills as a chiropractor. David then came back to work in England, and wrote a book, *Omens of Awareness*, which was an immediate success. It was a time of great learning for me – once I asked him about UFOs, and he said, 'When Man reaches a certain point of stagnation, he needs a huge shock and dramatic happening to make him move and open himself to new avenues of awareness.' He took the story of Elijah in the Bible being borne up in a fiery chariot, as a demonstration in those days, comparing it to a UFO, which certainly did give people a horrendous shock and spurred people to seek religion and a spiritual life. He points out that experiences of seeing UFOs are a new opening. He went on to practise for years, alas, not nearly as many as one would have hoped. He died young, a mere sixty, and he published many books on radionics which he then went into more and more. At one time we bought an instrument called the Mora instrument which was able to measure energy forces in the chakras and enable diagnosis of disease. He said this approach had the potential to revolutionise bio-energetic medicine and at the same time to establish an energy model of man that is spiritually based. He took as illustration in one of his books, *Subtle Energy*, Blake's marvellous picture of Perfect Man, with arms and legs outstretched, making the five points of the pentagon. David knew so many interesting people, and his mind was always on the move. He introduced me to Professor John Taylor, but he wanted to film me doing healing in my clinic and I was not prepared to do this without the full consent of my patients. For such a shy person David drew a lot of people to him during his life. He died because he was burnt out from all the energies which had flowed through his instrument, and I think that this is a lesson for many therapists to learn. We do not know how powerful the energy of a human being is, nor to what it extent it can also be damaged, and like the Curies, who died of cancer discovering X-Rays, so many of these new instruments are untested, but this is the risk that I think all healers with instruments take for the good of the cause. We had many interesting dialogues, shared and discussed our dreams and various cases we were treating – there is much to be gained by exchanges, especially of dreams. We worked together, he in one room and I in another at my home. He would send people to me for spiritual healing and I would send him those I thought he could help. One example of this was when we had a very difficult patient who was physically a problem, but the problem was also deeply psychological, and David had tried to help her for many weeks and then I tried to help her for many more weeks, also unsuccessfully. One day after this we got together and I said to David, 'You have one last go because I do not think I can help.' David came into my workroom beaming and said, 'You won't believe it – I had a huge breakthrough! You know, I helped her because I had completely given up, and in fact my energy and my help were not in the picture at all. What came, came through me and it went straight into her energy system and released the blocks.' I have so often found the same in healing. I've reminded myself over and over again, it is not us who does the healing – the patient does the healing. We are only the instrument through which it comes, and this is an important message.

David Tansley was a pilot light of our times. From a very profound level he communicated through his being a great light. When I first heard him lecture on radionics, I knew this was something important, as is the way with great communicators who are speaking from their souls. A carpenter has to have tools to do his work, but it is the will and spirit of the carpenter which does the best work, not the tools. During the years I knew David his work progressed as he grew. He was always ready to discard – because he was truly free – and to move on with his inner self, going on to new writing or new ways of practising. He created many radionic and homeopathic remedy instruments and was way ahead of his time. David's work was a landmark in radionics and a touchstone to further discoveries.

An extraordinary change was happening as time passed. To begin with, the people who wanted me to heal them had been suffering from physical diseases, including many common ones, and I found that healing gave them relief. Sometimes the medical condition itself did not change, but the person felt much better in themselves. I realised healing was working on the person's very being, not only on the body. I began to know without words what the problems were, or what to say. All the time I was learning and practising, and as I progressed, the type of patient coming to me changed. People came with psychological problems, whom I would not have been able to help if they had come earlier in my life. Though always my healing was done by laying on hands, now appropriate words sometimes came as well. I had more people with physical head or neck ailments. It seemed as if I was being sent people to help only as and when I was ready myself to help them. The experiences I had always seemed to come to teach me at just the right moment, and this has continued all my life. I do believe that we are sent suffering so that we can learn compassion for others.

So often in the evening I had one or two priests or doctors to simple supper to talk openly and privately about thoughts at soul level. This was always a joy, and productive, ironing out many problems and queries, learning more from each other. I thought often of the words: 'When one or two are gathered together in my name, I am with you.'

Also surely this was real communion – sharing of bread and wine while talking about spiritual things. It was important at a time when this sort of thing was considered by the Church to verge on witchcraft that these people could come in confidence and talk from their hearts without fear.

By this time I had moved to a much smaller home in Chelsea. My daughters had grown up and were on their own, though we always met at Uppark at weekends.

Then I met another interested doctor, the famous homeopath Dr Lambert Mount. Lambert Mount was a very spiritual person, and immensely compassionate and caring. One patient replied when I asked if she felt better, 'Of course I do, just being here with you and Doctor Mount in your healing home.' When we detach ourselves from the material world and all conditioned things as much as we can, healing emanates from all of us. Dr Mount asked me to dowse for the homeopathic remedies he used. The doses came to extraordinary quantities and strengths, quite unlike the usual – but Lambert had the courage and trust to go ahead, with quite miraculous results. He wanted to set up a clinic in Harley Street with me but as neither of us wanted to do the paperwork involved in research, the idea folded. He was an explorer and always on the search for better cures. He was intensely interested in life but alas was to die young – killed by a patient. His enquiring mind made me delve further into Christianity. He himself followed a religion called Subud – an Eastern teaching – and of course we found almost total common ground.

To further my knowledge and having been inspired by visits to Vézelay and to Spain I undertook a pilgrimage.

Pilgrimage is defined in the dictionary as a journey to a sacred place, or a long search made for exalted or other reasons – isn't this the passage of life itself?

I became aware of this journey when I was at convent school. Every three years, the school produced a performance of Bunyan's *Pilgrim's Progress*. This must be the greatest allegorical tale of life there is. The actors were chosen on merit rather than acting ability, and though rather wayward, I was amazed to be chosen as one of the shining ones at the gate. I only said three words but being chosen for this part has stuck forever. The Shining One also has to go through the dark and a pilgrim must be prepared for this and must be free of surplus luggage. This is a hard task in today's world.

At the time I was told a story …

… a man once had a dream in which he was fleeing flood waters with many others and climbing up a mountain. Everyone was carrying what they could in baskets and bags on their shoulders and on wheels. The man found himself beside a beautiful young woman with a handcart piled high. He helped her for a while, but the slope got steeper and it became obvious the cart would have to be abandoned. 'Leave some of your things,' he said. She threw off some possessions, but changed her mind and replaced them carefully. The waters rose and he was worried. She kept changing her mind and would not leave anything behind, nor abandon her cart, so he had to decide to go on without her, to freedom. This dream had an important message for the man …

I made the pilgrimage – not all on foot – to the holy place of Santiago de Compostela in Spain. I wanted to do this to reinforce my prayers for my late husband. I knew when I left his grave in Spain that he was at peace, but prayers should always be kept alive. I set off from England with friends to motor slowly across France to Vézelay in Burgundy. This most beautiful place was built in the middle ages on a high hill on a rock where there was a grotto in which were kept relics of St Mary Magdalene. Over the rock, a Cathedral of Light was built and at its feet the village grew down the hill. There were narrow, cobbled streets and beautiful medieval houses, many with the pilgrim's shell set in the doorway. Here, pilgrims knew they could find hospitality and deeper teaching.

The sign of a pilgrim was a shell (Coquille St Jacques), and these the pilgrims of old had sewn into their cloaks; sometimes the shells were made of lead to make the journey harder. The cloak would have been heavy and thick and would be used for sleeping in on cold nights if lodgings

Vézelay – Pilgrim's rest

could not be found. He carried a stick to fend off robbers and get through wild places, and a leather pouch for such food as he could beg. It was only on completion of the pilgrimage that he could wear the shell in his broad brimmed hat. He had to learn to tell his way by the stars, especially the pole star, and to know the signs he would find on certain houses, indicating they were safe for food and rest.

On arrival at Vézelay, my feet almost flew up the hill to the wonderful cathedral, bathed in a pink light from the setting sun. The powerful feeling evoked by many ardent pilgrims was clearly felt.

Pilgrim's shell coquille St Jacques

After a few days rest, the journey continued down through France, stopping at places where there were the same medieval houses, always with the sign of the shell. These were mostly of the fairly well-to-do burgher types – presumably people who could always afford to feed a hungry pilgrim. By the time I got to the Pyrenees to cross into Spain I was with another group of pilgrims. The thought of people walking over these vast mountains made me realise how spoilt we were. Even in the mountains there were pilgrims' lodgings, and one place had shells covering the entire walls. Travelling on into Spain the route grew harder, much of it still cobbled, until finally the last hill before Santiago was reached.

It was awesome indeed – there below in the distance lay the magnificent buildings of the cathedral and the square, on one side of which was the Hostel of the Catholic Kings. This had been built by the king and queen of Spain to house pilgrims newly arrived in the city. It is a huge building of small cells, each opening onto cloisters which formed a central square, in the middle of which was a fountain. Imagine the feelings of the pilgrims, some of whom had travelled years to their holy destination – fulfilled and free to rest. It still feels a very holy place, of course, though the hostel is now a hotel with modern comforts. The pilgrim's next act was, and still is, to enter the cathedral and visit the statue of Santiago (St James'), where he sits clothed in a bejewelled silver cloak. People file round the back of the statue and wrap their arms around his shoulders, a symbolic and evocative act. Some pilgrims would never return home, dying on the way or continuing life elsewhere. Some returned with an altered awareness of life. I know that I felt I had achieved a further step on my pilgrimage through life, and acquired a great deal more knowledge on the way – not only about places but also people. It is when you make a journey as a pilgrim that you begin to know yourself and others on a deeper level. Mostly we do not allow ourselves the time to do this, but remembering all those pilgrims and their journeys to Santiago de Compostela makes one pause for thought, and this may lead to a pause in which to be really still. Without stillness none of us can travel further along our way.

CHAPTER TEN

Uppark and the National Trust

Uppark – Robin Fedden and Bobby St John Gore – National Trust (NT) – Teresa Hale – Sarah Fetherstonhaugh – Emma – Mrs McCallum – Pete – Scotland – Clergymen

RETURNING TO UPPARK, a challenge awaited me as usual. By 1967 my mother-in-law moved out. She left Uppark in a helicopter, the modern equivalent of a broomstick, saying she would brush the dust off her feet. She never came back to the house, but she haunted the village and neighbours, sowing seeds of a destructive kind and generally making my life hard. She poisoned the beginning of what was to be a new era for me. I went from London to the empty house to stay for two nights, just to make sure I could deal with the energy there. It was cold, dark and most uncomfortable. I chose a spare bedroom with a four-poster bed, a hard seventeenth-century mattress made of compressed straw and on top a huge feather mattress which took four people to shake up. Beds of this age were made for shorter people, and the blankets were so stiff I couldn't move, but huddled in my fur coat with my faithful Peke puppy I slept. During the night I awoke to hear sounds of a great party going on downstairs. I knew it was Sir Harry. They were all having a happy time and I felt the house full of people enjoying life. Then I knew all would be well. There was no trace of previous occupants of Uppark other than Sir Harry and his mother Sarah. It was their house and others had come and gone in it like wisps of air. The room I occupied was called the Red Room and was requested for in letters from Prinny, later George IV, to Sir Harry when he was about to visit. It had an atmosphere charged with a heavy negative vibration – as if there had been unhappiness or more likely drunkenness and dissolute behaviour there. It had at one time been Sir Harry's bedroom, perhaps that was why. At times this heavy feeling pervaded the house. Anyone living there and inclined to negative energy was always affected. The only room which was unaffected was the Blue

Drawing Room upstairs that had been Emma Hamilton's room. I think her happy disposition overcame it. It had been after that Sarah Fetherstonhaugh's room – when I returned briefly to live there in 2000 she certainly was around and very gentle and beautiful.

I began to rearrange the house. I moved up the smaller and more beautiful things. Each child had a little bedroom with the most beautiful view in England. It was so exciting to find plaster relief (bronze) plaques over the dining room doors – made by my ancestor George Garrard. There was also a horse picture by Sawrey Gilpin, whose daughter married a Garrard, and bronze busts by Garrard of his patron, the Duke of Bedford. And here was I in the twentieth century woven back into the tapestry of Uppark. The house was all tatty, almost derelict like Sleeping Beauty's castle. I had to cook on a Calor gas stove in the housemaid's cupboard on the back stairs for months, while a bathroom, WC and kitchen were created out of large cupboards. I was told by a National Trust architect that a bathroom was impossible in such a space, but I went and bought the bath and WC and basin and got the workmen to carry them up and place them where I had imagined they could go. And I made the architect come and have a look to demonstrate how I was able to bathe.

Robin Fedden and Bobby Gore (R. St John Gore), pillars of the NT, dear friends and great fun, used to come down and approve of my arrangements. We would have what Robin called a *fête champêtre* on the Saloon floor as usually the chairs were stacked somewhere else or were in the process of being moved. It was a good happy co-ordinated sharing, though they often left not having arranged anything and I was left with piles of valuables to put in place – Chinese vases and chairs, pictures, all had to be arranged and set in order. We all enjoyed it so much too. The girls were growing up and had dinner parties and lots of room for people to stay. I owned a Pekinese called Tiggy for many years. He was very discriminating and jealous. A male friend arriving at the front door described three little girls with bright blue eyes holding a Pekinese and saying in chorus, 'This is Tiggy, he hates men.' He did hate men and bit anyone who came near me.

Some friends came for a party once and while we were having a drink in the drawing room, the Peke had gone through their suitcase in the spare room, selected a jewelled sandal and carried it off. I think my friend had to wear slippers to the dance. A long time later the Peke led me to the sandal, alas not in its original form. There was also a disaster as one couple Tiggy disliked came to stay, and each evening as the lady went to her bedroom, on the mat just in the middle of the doorway, Tiggy had left his worst kind of calling card to show his disapproval. I once had a charming letter from Bobby saying it had come to his notice that my Peke had a predilection for the gilded legs of the William Kent sidetables in the hall, so could I please change his habits as the gilt was going green.

After my dear friends Robin and Bobby left the Trust it became, for us, a much more impersonal and bureaucratic sort of affair, with inexperienced people appointed by the Trust in charge – a factory manager, a publican, a farmer – who generally lacked sympathy with the living nature of the house and showed little consideration to the family. Nor did they seem willing to listen or to learn. This was so sad because every family who had lived in the house learned what their predecessors did there, and all about them. This knowledge would have been easy to pass on, had they wanted to live with the place peacefully, though visitors loved talking to the family and having personal questions about Uppark life answered. They loved knowing how we lived and none of this was in the guide book. There always seemed to be a guided tour in action in the stone hall which had to be negotiated when the family came downstairs hauling the school trunk to get it into the car. They seemed to find these incidents more diverting than the dates of the paintings on the walls. They also enjoyed seeing a dolls' pram and gumboots inside the door. We all lived in the house until my eldest daughter Harriet married in 1969. When she had children I moved out and went to live in the gardener's cottage built in the wall of a walled garden in the park – a magical place.

While I lived there, my friend Teresa Hale came to stay. I first met Teresa when she came to me for healing. It was so marvellous then to find a young person who was so like-minded and with whom I could discuss all kinds of ideas about our visions of healing and the spiritual and all kinds of medical practice coming together eventually. Teresa was a brilliant administrator and had a business head, which I had not. She very efficiently put together a team of people each doing their own therapy under one umbrella. Later on I worked one day a week for Teresa in her clinic at Harley House, and eventually when her clinic was much larger she established it as the Hale Clinic and moved near to Regent's Park where it now flourishes. These days, the Hale Clinic is internationally recognised and therapists who have worked there can be sure to find work elsewhere. Teresa has often been the first to find out about a new complementary therapy going on and then, making sure of its integrity, has added it to her work. She has a very accurate spiritual awareness, not only of the uses of the therapies, but also of the practitioners who use them, so to pass Teresa's test of scrutiny is a significant achievement! This is why her clinic is visited by the rich and famous as well as thousands of others. Her reputation is the most trusted of any I know, and I greatly admire Teresa's focus on the vision she has held for so many years. She is also a wonderful yoga teacher and I remember her showing a brilliant yoga exercise, which involved being animals, to my grandchildren, who were enchanted by her when she stayed at Uppark.

Years later when my youngest daughter Sophie married, she moved into the walled garden cottage, and I returned to the attic of the big house. There I had a bed-sitting room with dormer windows and a huge view, but sadly far away from the ground and garden.

When I lived in Uppark there were times when I reflected on the general picture of life and wondered what I was doing there, and as in answer to my thoughts this came into my head ... Life is like a tapestry, we each of us are weaving – some of us have begun to see the overall pattern and why we have had to work on our own particular part, eventually to join one whole. We first see the outline and the shape and then fill in with many colours.

I had a vision of each person as a small candle – like birthday candles – and along came a great wind and all the candle flames joined into one huge light – is this how it will be? Later when in London this was demonstrated in St James's Church, Piccadilly at a service. Each person held a candle – the first in front had their candles lit from the altar and passed on the flame to light the one behind. The flames finally lit all the candles which were raised in an invocation – a most moving sight – making one huge, whole light that filled the church.

Once a very amusing incident happened when going through the heirlooms in the house – I turned out a huge Meissen soup tureen full of old lavender to show someone the mark underneath and out fell a set of my father-in-law's teeth. He hated them and used to slip them out whenever possible, usually popping them into his coat pocket but he must have been without a pocket when he did it this time. My mother-in-law loved dressing up as if she lived in olden days, and when I first stayed she expected me to put on a long dress for dinner, which I had not taken with me, so she dressed me up in her court dress, a silver and gold brocade dress with a diamanté collar and a train. I wore it once only, feeling such a fool. I was very upset but it has nearly worn out it has had so much use in the family fancy dress box in the attic. What a hamper there is in the attic and what a lot of fun and acting we had with it. Again part of history and heritage is the fancy dress box; what tales it could tell. I myself always loved dressing up and understood the need to be other than oneself as a child. In fact, though not dressed up I always acted a part when showing people around the house – changing myself depending on the audience.

Then followed a marvellous time rearranging the house. I opened up the old east front door. When I asked Robin, who was in charge at the time, if I might open it up as it originally had been, because I had seen it in the Tilleman picture, he said with his wonderful stammer, 'Y-y-yes my-y d-d-dear, d-do,' and cut out the drive to a size suitable for a horse and carriage to be able to sweep round to the door. My friend Pete was staying and he leapt on to the tractor and swirled round as if in a horse and carriage, ploughing up the turf. How pretty and welcoming that front door was and how much coming and going through it. It faced east and got the sun until midday, so many happy pre-luncheon drinks on the steps and joyful arrival of friends. The front door was gloomy. I decided to let the NT show people the whole of the ground floor, so that they could arrive at the front door like visitors, and we would use the back stairs and live on the first floor and the attic behind the baize door.

I felt a most essential part of the purpose of the opening of the house to the public was that the people who came wanting to show their families other people's houses, of the past and how people lived in them, should be treated as guests of the family. People could walk around all the ground floor rooms. I had a complete bedroom moved down and subsequently found through letters in the muniment room that it had originally been downstairs. Sir Harry's bedroom – no doubt so he could reach it without stairs.

History is made by people – no amount of conservation of houses will be of interest if the families who lived in them are omitted from their history and their present-day lives. The enjoyment shown by visitors whenever they met the family in the garden was immense. A party of French people, all of whom owned châteaux, only wanted to know the family history and how our ancestors could have been related. One visitor was heard to say going through the hall, 'Cor, look, they've got a dog's bowl,' as if it was not possible for people who lived like this to have anything so humble. Little did they know. Another was heard to observe what he thought of the white and gold drawing room, 'Not very comfortable I should say, they ain't got one decent chair.' A party of highly cultured Americans said it was quite the nicest of all the houses they were shown as it had gumboots, prams and coats in the front hall. Then they met us! They were far more interested in how we lived in the private flat upstairs and in all my grandchildren than in all the treasures.

At that time, someone who was very much a part of life at Uppark died. My very nice Scots farm manager McCallum was diagnosed with cancer and died. This was a terrible loss because he really had worked with me and for me in such harmony and we understood each other. It was a sad disaster and meanwhile his widow and her sheepdog had nowhere to go so I suggested that she came and lived with us. She came and lived in London for some time (while I worked on Uppark still), which was very courageous of her because she was very much a country woman. As soon as it was possible, she moved back to Uppark into the attic and stayed with us for many years. It was really thanks to Mrs McCallum that I was able to get on and make a home of the first floor and arrange everything for my family. She held the fort during the week while I was in London, and cooked marvellous meals for us at weekends at Uppark. Her photograph is on show with others in Uppark now.

At this time I had a very special friend, Peter. We had met in London but his home was in the Highlands and so I think was his heart. He was the most wonderful mixture of interests and abilities. Among other things, he had done a spell as barman at the Ritz and was a master chef. He had owned a ballet company and been involved in theatre. He was intelligent and well read and best of all had, like me, childish ideas and could laugh more than anyone. Though he had a London house and took part in London life and parties he spent most of his time in Scotland. His house was in a dream place in the Highlands, on the edge of a loch and very remote. The light in the Highlands is exceptional anyway, but there it seemed unreal. The sky was so beautiful all the time and the colours were brighter and always changing – seeing it was a peak experience – when something seems so beautiful one is transported out of this world. It cannot be explained as it is gone before one has formed words to describe it. I have had other such experiences into glimpses of heaven. I stayed a lot with Peter, always busy creating some fantastic folly. He was the most enjoyable companion, a wonderful friend and a very attractive person with whom I could share my life. I found sharing my feelings difficult – people often seemed rather shallow to me and not prepared to discuss things at soul level – unlike Pete. It was a very romantic romance – he was romantic looking too, in his kilt in the right surroundings. We spent days once climbing up to a rock cleft down which he poured glue, then bags and bags of coloured sequins – imagine what hoary old kilted sportsmen with guns shooting grouse must have thought when they came across this. One day I left my three precious children with him and when I got back I saw them in the middle of the loch on a raft he had made from a door – lashed on to three empty oil drums. This shocked me; I was horrified and realised I could not happily leave him with my children. Pete often came to stay at Uppark as he was very artistic and full of ideas – he helped us so much. Sadly, in the end our ways had to part. It wasn't possible to combine my children at their various schools and in their growing up life and London, and manage Uppark and live in Scotland. Pete quite understandably could not live his life at Uppark. Sometimes in life one has to make painful decisions – this was one of them, but to go back to the happy times we had at Uppark there followed a marvellous period rearranging the house.

One of the duties, I was appalled to discover, that went with living at Uppark was Patron of the Living. This is a very old custom which I think dated back to the middle ages. The local landowner was Patron of the Living in the parish of Harting. There had been a very nice, very ordinary clergyman while my parents-in-law were there, who my father-in-law had known in the navy. He had either died or retired, so I was told that I was to interview prospective vicars for the village. It was rumoured that my father-in-law had caused the last vicar to have a heart attack because he was told to come and admonish me for sending my daughter to a Rudolf Steiner school; worse than admonish, forbid me, to send her. This was dangerous ground, so the vicar had the job. Neither my parents-in-law nor the vicar had heard of anthroposophy, nor of course of Steiner. They imagined it was some kind of occult sect and, as I had always felt my mother-in-law was something of a witch, using black energies, this was powerful stuff. I acted swiftly. I was advised by the Steiner school to give the vicar a passage from one of their books to read what was probably Steiner's interpretation of the gospels. The vicar was a good man. He read this and the subject was never spoken of again.

I had studied Steiner's work with my husband and together we had found it very interesting and, very revealing. Richard started to try and farm organically because of this study.

I asked the Bishop of Chichester why interviewing was my role, and he said, 'Well, I don't want you to worry about that, but I would just like you to see them and talk to them and give me your honest opinion of them as a person,' and obviously if it was a person who I felt would be suitable as a clergyman in the village. So in due course a clergyman turned up at teatime, which I felt was a good time, and we had a talk. He was a tall very good-looking man, with absolutely snow white hair. The sort of introductory chit-chat was most unsatisfactory until I found he had been a missionary in Africa, and it explained why the gap was really very large between country life as I saw it in a village in England and his life as it had been in Africa. However, we ploughed on. It was very hard going and he obviously had not the slightest sense of humour and it was hard to find anything in common. I did say to him that I found life very difficult as a widow, and that I felt rather embarrassed at being asked to do this particular job and so on, and before I knew where I was he said, 'Well, let us pray,' and I realised that, as he had thrown himself on his knees with his face buried in the seat of his chair, I was expected to do the same. Somehow in the drawing room at Uppark it seemed slightly out of place. I do really know that one can pray absolutely anywhere and under any circumstances, but to me such a display of it didn't seem quite right and I remember thinking how embarassing, supposing someone comes in. However, they didn't, and after long prayers, mostly for me, he obviously didn't think I was a very suitable person to be Patron of the Living, we got up and he left. So my report to the bishop was not really very enthusiastic which he completely accepted.

Then came along another vicar and this one came with his wife, a voluble lady who answered all the questions for him. He hardly had a chance to get a word in, but he did come and sit next to me on the sofa, which as it happened was a bad move because of my Peke. Any man who came and sat with me was all right as long as he didn't put his arm out. I said to him, 'Whatever you do, don't touch my Peke,' and he appeared to take that in and nervously balanced his tea cup and had tea and so on. Then I felt I really had to know more about him, so I tried to talk to him and from sheer nerves he immediately put out his hand and tried to stroke the Peke, who sunk his teeth in his hand and drew blood. There was fearful confusion and I insisted he wash the wound. However, he was extremely amiable and appeared to make no complaint. By then it was about six, so I said, 'Oh, let's have a drink – I'm sure you need one,' and his wife leapt up and said, 'Oh no, we have a meeting. We absolutely must fly, we must get back.' So I said goodbye and saw them off. Much later, I was a bit worried because I felt there was something I had not quite got to the bottom of, and I asked my good friend the Archdeacon of Chichester about vicars and told him about this one and how he was bitten. He laughed and said, 'Well, he must have been very desperate to impress you – I knew him in the navy and if anything like that happened he was the greatest blasphemer of all time.' But anyway this time he certainly didn't let a word pass his lips. However, I asked an old friend to go over to the village where this vicar had come from and find out more about him and what the people thought of him. This good friend went and had a pint in the local pub. He chatted away and asked about their vicar, and then someone said, 'Ah, yes, he's a wonderful man, we love our vicar, he is very popular with us all and he comes in here every night and has his pint with us and passes the time of day, but something must have happened last week. He came in here late and had a great deal of something much stronger than a pint.' Poor man. Worse was to come – I gave a good report of him to the bishop because I liked him. He duly arrived to be interviewed by the parish council, alas, weaving his way up the path. Oh dear me, that was the end of him.

So then, trying again, I was asked to see another vicar, a bachelor, and this one I liked very much indeed and had high hopes for the future. His great worry was whether he could get his grand piano into the vicarage drawing room. I had visions of wonderful concerts in the church and every kind of possibility for musical life in the village. So we talked away and he seemed to me very holy, slightly overdressed for the village in a long black soutane, I thought, but anyway quite all right. So I sent a glowing report and showed great enthusiasm to the bishop but again this was not to be. The bishop said he had received an unsatisfactory report about him from somewhere else in the meantime, so no.

After that I really did lose heart, and declined to see the next few vicars or let the parish council see them first. Anyway no-one suitable was found and I think the vicar holding the fort in the village got fed up too. Eventually, I had a call from the bishop to say they had reconsidered the bachelor with the grand piano and he was to be appointed. So I was delighted and he was duly installed. I think I was away and I didn't see him for some time, then came the autumn and harvest festival. I think I was at one of the children's schools for the occasion, but later that week, to my absolute horror, my daily, Stella, who was really part of Harting village, said, 'Ooh, did you see about our local vicar on the telly?' My heart sank. The vicar felt that the church did not have enough flowers for the Sunday harvest festival. He had conducted a funeral the day before and had remarked to someone what a waste it was to leave such lovely flowers to die, and when the bereaved relatives visited the grave on the

Sarah Fetherstonhaugh

Monday, it had only bent wire and cards. It was sad for the family, but the vicar did show enterprise and made good sense in a way! But unfortunately, terrible umbrage was taken all round and it seemed to have caused such ructions that the next thing, our vicar was on his way out.

After that, and it took some years in the doing, I handed the Patronage of the Living back to the Bishop. I really felt, without any personal reason, that in this day and age and under the circumstances at Uppark, it was an outdated custom. My eldest daughter had married a Roman Catholic and so my eldest grandchildren would be Roman Catholic. The village was no longer a village. It consisted of a small part of the original village with the families who had lived in it for hundreds of years, but a large part of it was new private and council houses with new people in them. A lot of old cottages had been renovated as nice comfortable homes for retired admirals and their wives and weekenders. This made for a completely different population and church-going people to be catered for. In retrospect I wish I had not handed it back, but anyway, one can only do what feels best at the time.

All the life happening at Uppark was at weekends and school holidays – my children were either at boarding schools or on courses in London, so during the week it was London life.

CHAPTER ELEVEN

Roots of Spiritual Healing

Argyll Road – Embassy Parties – Kos – Conference on Spiritual Healing

So MUCH HAPPENED in these years on all levels, mostly at Argyll Road. It was such a beautiful large house, where so much was to happen – when the family and grandchildren came along, with healing work and when my clinic grew and different doctors began taking interest. It was where my spiritual knowledge was able to deepen and where I also had a lot of enjoyment at parties and concerts and with friends. I had several flirtations. I met a very attractive Persian ambassador at an embassy party. One evening he took me to the Iranian Embassy to show me some exquisite and very rare Persian miniatures. There were large plates of Turkish Delight everywhere and fantastic rugs. To show hospitality, he put a match to the perfectly-laid fire, and the paper fan lit up – the fire lit up, the chimney lit up and it soon became obvious that either the chimney was blocked or there never was meant to be a fire there. The whole embassy was full of billowing smoke – no alarms in those days past midnight. Windows and doors were unceremoniously flung open and normality returned. A premonition, perhaps of the dreadful terrorist siege later, when it was burned down. The handsome Persian was less attractive in daylight and not at all right for country life. Instead of flowers, he sent enormous tins of the best caviar but that didn't compensate for a black fedora and long coat at Uppark.

Often, when feeling tired, I wondered why I was going to a party. I didn't feel enthusiastic, but a kind of urge, almost a voice, would say: you must go. On those occasions, sure enough, one person would ask a question that led to a deeper level of thought, about either their beliefs or their troubles. They would ask to come to my healing centre, and from there, almost without fail, they would go on to find something in their search for a deeper meaning to their lives. It was as if healing acted as a catalyst or a touchstone. A very different friend was an Austrian prince, one of many impoverished but almost royal refugees from Eastern Europe living in England. His name was known all over Europe and acted like a passport, opening doors when I travelled. I took my children skiing every winter and his name, when he had telephoned ahead, soothed all problems and made life easier. Such a nice kind person. A friend said, 'Why don't you marry him, he would look after you, put the car away, let out the dogs and make the coffee at breakfast?' Then she said, 'No, upon reflection, he would leave the car lights on, lose the dogs and make the coffee in the percolator without putting in the coffee – better not you would be unkind.' The end of our romance was a sad little story. He wore squeaky boots that drove me mad. So I said, 'You should stick a drawing pin through the sole, then tread on it.' I learnt this trick from soldiers in the war – the drawing pin in the bottom of thick soles lets out the air and stops the squeak. The prince misunderstood and thought I was literally telling him to put a nail through his foot. Much later, my daughter at boarding school told me her friend's mother, a rich attractive widow, had a new boyfriend. But the friend said, 'He drives Mummy mad as he has squeaky boots ...' It was of course the same pair of boots.

One day some Swiss healers came to visit and invited me to take part in a congress on the Greek island of Kos, to be headed by Professor Arnold Kaserling, a leading shaman from Vienna. Kos is the site of the Temple of Asclepius and the birthplace of Hippocrates in the fourth century.

Naturally I was thrilled to be going to this conference entitled *The Common Roots of Medical and Spiritual Healing*. Hippocrates merged Greek and Egyptian healing traditions: from Egypt the five steps of mystical initiation, and from Greece the interpretation of dreams by Asclepius. The congress of ninety was attended by Germans, Austrians, French, Italians and a few English. The purpose was to study as a group and to re-establish our contact with the earth and healing through herbs, dreams and in other ways.

During the five days the steps were studied. Explained to us was the relationship between Judaism, the Essenes and Christianity, and then the connection in the fourth century between Asclepius and Christ, and other teachings on healing. It was in AD 545 that the Christian bishops forbade healing not given under the sanction of the Church or in its name. Later, the Church would again complain about people giving healing, when issues like these resurfaced in the 1960s, and it was only nearing the turn of the millennium that it became a normal part of many lives and well-known to many more. At that time, Hippocrates and others began to practise allopathic medicine. The five steps to healing were as follows:

The approach to the Temple of Asclepius, symbolising the recognition that help and healing are needed with a problem or illness or a dream.

The second step was purification through washing, as in the Christian baptism, and the casting off of everyday clothes and all mental burdens.

The third was meditation on questions of disease; self-examination and fasting to further cleanse body and mind; a waiting in silence.

The fourth step was to meet the Gods/Goddesses, and exchange gifts with them – a realisation of the gifts open to seekers of the truth, and giving and receiving, and integrating with God.

And the fifth step was the dream stage and learning the methods used. Explanations and information on the inner self from Asclepius would be received in a dream state, understanding reached – enlightenment.

The return journey down the steps of the temple was made with thanksgiving.

On the last night of the conference at midnight, the group went through this whole experience in silence, under a full moon, in the temple which was built on five levels. This was a truly magical experience. Each of us felt that we had received and understood healing during the past week.

Daily lectures were on various aspects and ways of healing and self-transformation, through homeopathy, trance and hypnotism and forms of transpersonal psychology. But it was ultimately for everyone to come to their own translation and application of the Hippocratic method of healing. I will say that some of the experiences and workshops seemed to me rather way-out and even violent, particularly those connected with shamanism and with some forms of hypnosis, but they were all voluntary. Some of them were marvellous and taught me things I have used ever since. The enormous value was the exchanging and sharing of information with people of all nationalities, all engaged in ways of healing. It made me realise how we really are each of us part of the whole, and how we are all one another and how essential communication is – even if not fully understood. A great sharing of the common experience brings much healing and expansion of vision, which can tend to become limited.

Of the exercises I learned there, two were very valuable and are as follows:

The first was a meditation given by a German homeopath. A roomful of people were to stand in a circle and each was asked to choose a note to hum. This was very interesting because some people who feel they are not musical find it quite hard to hum a note, but everyone can produce a hum or sound of some kind. This became evident as we all hummed to together, and each of us was to imagine the cycle of a flower, birth to death, humming all the while. The cycle of a flower from the seed, the root deep down in the earth, growing, pushing up, the little green knob coming up above the earth, growing, putting out leaves, growing taller, the flower itself in bud, opening, fully opening, stretching out its petals, emitting its scent, its colour, making the shape of its petals, and then in its perfect glory enjoying the light and sun. Then slowly fading away with its petals dropping off, crumbling, leaves drooping, sap receding and so dying and returning to the earth for recycling. The most extraordinary result was the harmonious musical sound that this produced – heavenly! Music of the Spheres.

A charming exercise also aimed at children was given.

Each child chooses to be a certain animal, and the animal goes on a journey, meeting other animals on the way. The person leading the exercise helps the children to imagine their journey as an animal, whatever it is, with encounters, and all the adventures an animal could have in a wood. This really calls upon a child's imagination which is always there but is often not allowed to expand. Also, it was taught to us that each animal will represent some trait in the child, and much can be learned from this.

It was a fascinating conference, and years later I went to stay with some friends I had made there who lived in Hydra. Though still Greece, Hydra had a very different feeling – jewels of small Orthodox churches and the spirit of past times were there. I made a German friend who subsequently helped me make the Frédéric Lionel video, and a Chinese lady who after visits to me in London began introducing five-minute meditations at the start of her board meetings. The board was running one of the largest hotel chains round the world and the idea spread.

CHAPTER TWELVE

Family Weddings

Family weddings – Uppark and the National Trust – Charlie

THE GRAND SALOON AT UPPARK never looked more beautiful than on these occasions. All the furniture was removed and I felt it probably had originally been designed as a room where people paraded up and down and enjoyed its beauty. Out of all the windows was the most beautiful view in England, and it was often above the clouds. The sea and the Isle of Wight could be seen in the distance, and turning inwards the white and gold ceiling shone and sparkled. The chandeliers must have looked breathtaking ablaze with candles.

In Sir Matthew's and Sir Harry's days the butlers would have placed the chairs around the walls and carried in breakfast tables to set in front of them, with trays of food and drink.

The dairy maid Mary Anne and Sir Harry were married in the saloon in 1825, and in the records there is a charming description of their wedding.

The next marriage was my daughter Harriet's in 1969 – her husband-to-be, John, was a Roman Catholic, but the marriage was allowed in Harting Church, with both Anglican and RC priests present. The reception was in the Saloon. The room was shimmering with light and full of flowers and friends. Then they drove away in romantic style in an open car, from the Saloon steps, over the lawn and away.

Then Emma married in 1976. Her husband-to-be, Geoffrey, understood numerology, and asked me which of two dates – Boxing Day or 3 January? I suggested the latter date. When the time came, there had been a hurricane for several days; trees blown over the drives, telephones down, electricity gone, etc. But on the morning of the wedding came a great calm. The sun shone all day – children played outside on the lawn. The following day, the hurricane took off again. They were married in the Red drawing room, and a happy reception once again was in the Saloon.

The wedding had not been allowed in church by the Bishop of

Chichester, because Geoffrey had been married for a year and divorced. Was this judgement by the Church really true Christianity? We are told in the Gospels to forgive – and much later after years of study I realised

Family wedding

that the present day practices of the Church have deviated a long way from the original teaching we were given.

Sophie was the last to marry, in 1985, also in the house, overflowing with flowers and at a beautiful service, so full of meaning. A great luncheon was held again in the Saloon before she and Angus drove away.

But by now things were very difficult at Uppark. Things were changing for the worse. The spirit of the house felt uncomfortable. The National Trust appointed a series of caretakers to look after it, but none had any real idea of how life in an ancestral home was lived, nor how it should be. Like all large, bureaucratic movements, they did not want to know how the house should be kept. Stories that had been passed from one generation to the next were dismissed, and no-one wanted to learn, nor to know.

Meanwhile, and for years ahead, I had to struggle with lawyers, accountants and valuers to pay the astronomical death duties owed. Chattels had to be valued and sold to the estate duty, who passed them on to the National Trust, creating enormous amounts of paperwork and though the chattels, furniture and pictures remained *in situ* in the house where they were viewed by the public, they were no longer ours. Caretakers lived in their own department, mentally and physically, and stuck by their own rules – no account was taken of family life. Shutters were clanged shut summer and winter, lights turned off, and out-of-season furniture, instead of looking beautiful and asleep, was stuffed into hideous dust covers, like palls on coffins. The house was made to seem not sleeping, but dead, except for vibrant life going on upstairs where the family lived.

At this much later date of 2001, things have fortunately changed for the better. The family have a happy relationship with the present custodian and the atmosphere is very harmonious and enjoyable.

On 25 May 1972, there was joyful news – Charlie arrived. Harriet and John's new son was the first of my seven grandchildren. The moment I saw him at a few hours old, I knew he was very special. There was such an amazing light around him – he was like a little candle and somehow he showed me a whole new vision of the future, like looking down an avenue of beautiful trees towards a vast light ahead. He brought a most special healing with him, which he emanated wherever he was and to whoever he was with. He had such a hard journey ahead – he became diabetic and lived a life dependent on painful injections and measured food – often rushed to hospital in a state of crisis, but always seemingly happy and cheerful. Never have I met anyone who had to suffer so many disappointments so often and who was so swift to recover. Charlie was an enchanting little boy – very early on he called me Guggy, which I have been ever since. I was able to enjoy his company for one day a week – first in his Moses basket and then on his feet. We had such a very close relationship without even having to speak. How I loved those walks with the big pram – large hood and large sprung wheels – and Charlie sat high up facing me – not at car exhaust level – so we could converse. Sometimes he would lie in the garden and watch the sun glinting through the trees, and see the leaves rustling and in autumn fluttering down. Do today's parents know what their children are missing? There are things far better than cars, radios etc. When pushed in a pram, all the beautiful, harmonious things provided all around us by nature can be seen – yes, in towns too, for I had Charlie in London and at Uppark. Each stage of his life was to me an agony and an ecstasy – whenever he was hypo, as he often was, I always felt the same gut fear of his death; like I did when Richard had his asthma attacks; but the ecstasy and joy of his companionship was so valuable – my whole life changed. I suddenly felt that all the struggle and toil were worth it for his future – everything took on a different perspective. Other grandchildren came along through the years, but after many years I began to think that maybe the time had come to move away a bit and not be breathing down the family's necks. So I moved to the gardener's cottage in the magic walled garden. I had the most enjoyable time with my grandchildren – seeing them every week and during all the holidays – growing up through many stages of achievement. All the fascinating questions asked kept me endlessly asking myself the answers for as we answer a child, we should be very sure of what we say – words, once spoken, stick.

I was once told by a beautiful old lady that Charlie was a child lent by angels and lowered in a basket to us – from time to time they would give the string a tug which they did, until suddenly the time came for them to take him back – which they did when he was twenty-four years old. He had perfect musical pitch, and I am sure he is singing with angels still. I always had to be very careful not to create a conflict of ideas between me and his parents. I found this very hard sometimes – Charlie had a Catholic father and there were lots of queries I avoided answering as I could not have been honest.

When Charlie was sixteen and at Downside School, which felt like a medieval institution, he said, 'You know, Guggy, it's very hard. I can't always really believe what I'm told to believe without asking questions, which we're not allowed to do.' My tongue was tied but I was diplomatic. I believe freedom of thought is vital. When Charlie's sister Maria arrived, they had a very strict old nanny once a week, who was not nice to Charlie (I always felt she was jealous of our relationship) and used to say at meals, 'Charlie, sit up.' When he came to me one day he asked if he could get down and eat his lunch under the table. 'Of course,' I said. I always let my grandchildren do as they wish, on condition that they don't do it anywhere else, so he had his lunch under the table. One day as a very small boy he took the place opposite me at lunch and said, 'Guggy, I think I take the place of my grandfather for you.' How perceptive – he just knew things. He used to lie with his head at the bottom of his little four-poster bed because, he said, he could talk with his grandfather when he went to bed. It had been Richard's bed as a child. This inner seeing

Charlie

and hearing I quite understood and believed. Charlie had a vocation as a healer, for sure. At school, when I used to stay nearby and visit him, he would introduce special friends – what a number of cups of tea I consumed. They were only allowed to talk with me one by one, and what questions I was asked. I tried my best to answer without destroying a structure that had to be left intact for the time being – yet I had to be honest. Thinking beyond religion, time, space, into a cosmic dimension, we are all one and this is interpreted in all religions.

We had such a lot of laughter too. Charlie's vocation he felt was to be a doctor – he struggled for so long and so hard, but exams were too difficult. He went to nurse children in a hospital in Jerusalem – there he was in his element. Not only with the sick children, but with all the people he met. He was a wonderful listener, and made friends with Jews and Arabs and said he saw both sides. He participated in private Jewish family festivals as the only outsider. He went to meals with Arabs in their homes. Charlie was a party-lover too, musical and a good dancer – what a great life! I think when he got a job as a water keeper and river watcher in the Outer Hebrides, he was happiest of all. In his letters he wrote that he felt he had really found himself. I know he really appreciated the magical beauty – unique colours, crystal air and water – he was removed from the pressure and pollution in the south. Our flights of fancy together were like two birds, soaring above the clouds, but alas, not always practical. He must have had so many disappointments. He expected so much of himself and his diabetes always seemed to strike at the most unwanted moments – he must, underneath his happy exterior, have had much frustration for someone with so much to offer, but within the strictures of the 'real' world, was not able to bring his ideas to fruition. And then suddenly, one dreadful day in February 1997, Charlie was dead. I felt the light had gone out – mine had – again, as when Richard died that night, my room was filled with the most miraculous violet light which I see when a great healing takes place. I saw a wonderful light – a heavenly light. Charlie knew this too. We often had discussions at soul level which is important, and is when one has to re-examine all one's thoughts and almost do homework. As I said to my remaining grandchildren, Charlie had gone from us to make the light lighter.

The Polish army priest at the hospital where I nursed in the war, Father Andrew Glazewski, said after his death through a medium, 'The ecstasy of dying is something I can never, never express. It is suddenly like becoming light itself. It is so wonderful. It is heat and coolness. It is warmth in the mind. It is a clarity of vision and understanding. It is like a clap of Divine Thunder and hey presto! There I am out of my body leaping about in the glorious ether, you have no conception of what dying is like. It is a communion, a sacrament of living on a higher level ... the most transforming experience any mortal can attain. I am overcome with Joy, just Joy.'

I feel sure this is how Charlie will have experienced it. His smile alone touched so many people's lives that I think we only realised by the tributes and attendance at services for him afterwards, how many people he affected, but as was remarked by another of the family, 'When the leader of the pack is dead, the next one takes over.' We none of us should forget that we have to learn to accept the unacceptable to be free.

CHAPTER THIRTEEN

Travel and the Crystal Skull

USA, California – Crystal Skull – Bach Flowers – Ireland: fairy stories, stone circles, Paddy Rossmore, Galway Bay – Stonehenge – Father Felix – Iona

IT WAS DURING THE 1970s that I made many short journeys brought about because of queries in my reading. As with people I met who introduced me to other like minds, one book led to another, and these prompted questions that needed answering. One such journey was to the USA. Flying over the North Pole I realised what a very small grain of sand I was. It was a life changing experience. On arrival in California I was warmly greeted by friends in their house near the beach. Bliss, I thought, but when I wandered off to lie in the sun I was followed by a butler in white gloves with a sun brolly, lilo, thermos of iced water, orange juice and all – no peace and the fascinating pelicans flew away. Another morning gazing out to sun and sea, suddenly a torrent of water drenched the view and went on for half an hour. I realised this was mechanical watering and happened at regular weekly intervals. I felt like Alice in Wonderland, sometimes so large I could not reduce my size to enter, sometimes so small I felt like an ant. Shopping in the supermarket was a nightmare – so big – so much – so fast. Being driven on the roads in a car the size of a bus was the same without the diversion of villages by the roadside, but I was able to get to the Crystal Skull. While working in my clinic, I heard talk of a magical crystal skull. It was purported to have been discovered in 1925 by a Canadian in the ruins of Mayan pyramids. It had been so finely carved no-one could find by what means or tools. It was thought to have been used for divination purposes, as an oracle. While Frank Dorland, the engineer with whom I stayed in California, had the skull in his house, very strange things came about – unnatural movement of furniture, weather conditions, abnormal functions in his finely tuned instruments and so on.

It was swiftly returned to its owner. Since my visit in 1976, the crystal skull has come to public notice and been written about and televised, but at the time it was mind-blowing because of its strange power and secrecy, and still is. There are others too around the world. This visit took me back to Mexico and those strange and powerful pyramids set in the jungle. They were larger than one could imagine and quite overpowering, built for no discernible reason, but with many references to the sun. Many of their ceremonies were bloodthirsty of course, and here, as on ancient Irish sites where energies had been manipulated, they were powerful and dark. I often found solace in Christianity, in a chapel or abbey wherever I was. The Mayans were a civilisation who left nothing of themselves, only their history in puzzling mosaics and hieroglyphs, uncovered from great depths in some of these huge buildings. In the markets many herbs were sold, and the sellers would make a diagnosis of your ailment that was amazingly correct. They would describe the inner temperament of the patient. Our Indian guide's granny had been a renowned herb healer and herbalist, and I wanted to stay and study. But the energy of the crystal skulls was confirmation enough of the power of dowsing and crystals, which I had found so reliable. All this is ancient knowledge, and slowly we are rediscovering it.

When I returned to my clinic, I became even more involved in the Dr Bach flower remedies, and their potency and effect on the whole person. I took them to France later on, and translated their uses into French for Paul Geley, a healer I was working with in Burgundy. I discovered that many elderly people living in isolated places knew all that Dr Bach had discovered and of course they used herbs.

At home there followed work conferences with crystals, dreams and also using colour, which I had begun to study in the work of Rudolf Steiner. These were all tools in my bag if needed, but my hands were always first. I made many short journeys in pursuit of the answer to some query that had cropped up – Ireland and fairies was next.

My travels in Ireland led me to a great deal more learning about healing, in a round-about way. Ireland really was special. My husband was Irish and my father-in-law told me that the Meade family came from the bogs of Ballynatubagh way back in the dark ages. I think this could have probably been true but they ended up living north of the border and married Protestants. What often happened in Ireland was that the Irish families in the south became very impoverished and after the eighteenth century, when the Anglo-Irish took root and the rich English came over and settled with their money as Protestants, a lot of the poor

Catholic Irish from the south went north and married rich Protestants. This caused an even greater mixture; Ireland had always been a mixture.

I set off because suddenly I was inspired to collect fairy stories. I think stories are very important, and story telling is something that is fading out. People don't generally sit down and tell their children stories, nor do we have story telling among a group any more. It is an important thing because it enables the preservation of legends and myths which have a lot of information in them and were used as teachings as well as enchantment. It is wonderful and valuable to remain in touch with the mythical. So, very keen to record fairy stories, I set off for Ireland with a tape recorder. I laughed so much afterwards, because my whole trip to Ireland was a series of fairy stories. I certainly didn't record anything, but my memories of Ireland have been most profitable and varied, and allowed me even more stories to tell my grandchildren. The great thing I realised in Ireland after a little while was not to say one came from London, England, but to say I was Scots and grew up just over the water down in the south-west of Scotland. This immediately created a link and a bond – important because I found the Irish were not willing to have a crack, or a tale as they say, until they knew what they wanted to know about you first. If you came from Scotland, you passed muster, and they said you were practically related. Driving along was a wonderful experience, you never knew which way you were going, all the signposts were written in Irish, and as I don't speak or read Irish it was quite impossible. Frequently, too, the signposts were pointing in the opposite direction where they had been turned round by some mischievous imp. But if you stopped to ask a man the way, he would tell you with great confidence to follow the road straight ahead and take the turn on the right where there were two trees, and then if you went along another ten minutes or so, you came to a letterbox and turned left. After another little way along, you were to go over a hill and down into the next valley and along there you would find three turns on the right which would take you to the village you were searching for. This turned out to be a great myth, a fairy story, and you never arrived. It happened so often that I was puzzled. I remarked to an Irish friend on how strange this was, and he laughed and said, 'Ah yes, but you see the Irish always like to please, and rather than say sorry I have no idea, they'd rather tell you a way because they feel it is nice to be able to help you and be able to give you at least something, even though it might not be the right way.' Quite a charming idea unless one happens to be in a hurry, but then it's not so good to travel in Ireland if time is at all a factor.

Early Christian Cross, Ireland

I stayed sometimes with friends and sometimes in most amusing and derelict hotels which had been someone's ancestral home and which had been taken over by enterprising people – not always comfortable but certainly entertaining. Food was delicious and usually the view or the surroundings were beautiful. I had a friend in Dublin, a charming man and my idea of what a leprechaun might look like, small, very energetic and bright-eyed. He was the Dublin museum photographer and there for many

Ireland

an hour I listened to him telling how these wonderful ancient treasures had been dug from the bogs of Ireland. In fact I was allowed to handle a chalice (that still had the peat on it) which was dated about AD 400. The amazing thing was that he told me the wonderful filigree work on some of these gold objects and jewellery could not be copied nowadays because we don't have fine enough precision instruments. What must the people of those days have been like? They may have lived rough but the work they created was stunning and somehow it really did something for one's deepest feelings to actually hold an object of such inspired beauty.

After Dublin I drove on and made various visits, once to the Holy Wells, to dowse the content of the water. At the same time I was doing some very extraordinary work with an engineer on the energies in stone circles. The water in the Holy Wells was well-known for healing properties for specific ailments and it became evident after a while that the wells, for example, that were supposed to cure eyes had a very high content of silver. Silver is often included in eye remedies. The wells known for liver cures had high amounts of sulphur, and so on. Actually it wasn't just a meaningless myth – I was given a list of the possible water contents of wells and sometimes had to go a long way to get to it but it always made sense.

The research in stone circles was a very big work which took over a period of three years with many visits to and fro, not all the time but just in spurts. I went and stayed with a friend, Paddy Rossmore, who lived just near the border. A very Irish Irishman who lived in his keeper's house on his own estate near his ancestral home, once a castle which had now tumbled down and was then in ruins. But Paddy was very happy in his keeper's house in the woods. It was quite a spooky place but nevertheless great fun. I went on to stay with the engineer, Jim, I was working with over the border. Once Jim came to fetch me by car from Paddy's house, and somehow something delayed my departure. A rather strange conversation took place and then a goodbye to Paddy which seemed rather out of place and unreasonable. This delayed us for a few minutes and saved our lives. Jim drove his wife and me over the border and as we approached, a terrible thing happened. A soldier with a rifle faced us in the road, screaming, 'Go back! Turn around! Get off the road!' and bits of mud and glass and blood were flying everywhere on to the car. This was the day Lord Mountbatten was killed on the other side of Ireland and in front of us an army vehicle and eighteen soldiers had just been blown up and all were killed. This was a real shock and I felt here one was very near to a most terrible problem which one can't imagine unless one sees it with one's own eyes and experiences the appalling suddenness of it. Anyway, we turned aside and as my host lived there he knew side lanes and so we got back to where we were staying. That really was an insight into the darker side of Ireland – like Spain, both have this darkness of history and a magic about them too. Always it has been so – I was again doing healing work with great positive energies in a place where such terrible negative things were occurring. One seems to draw the other, black and white, yin and yang. We did a lot of work in a very little known stone circle called Ballynoe, and this circle did have very powerful healing vibrations. We wanted to find how these energies were used. It is a very long story – among other things we found that the stones emanated alternating positive and negative, male and female, energies, which spiralled. We presumed that groups of highly initiated people standing in these circles had been able to manipulate energies along the ley lines out of these circles to special places. We usually found the energy lines later. We also almost always outside many stone circles found what was called the heal stone, or helio. We called it the healing chamber because it seemed that under this place, outside the same circle, there would be an underground chamber. Perhaps people were put into this chamber to receive healing ... how little we really know. But people have actually carried this out since. I myself have, not actually putting anyone in the healing chamber but by putting someone into a healing stone circle in Ireland (it was someone who really was dying of cancer) and they made a miraculous recovery. What was this mysterious energy? Who knows?

One evening we had been dowsing in the circle, and Jim took me to my lodgings in the darkness, and as we stood at the front door he seemed to become rather strange. I didn't know whether it was because he was embarrassed at leaving me (he and his wife had no room for me to stay with them), or what, but he was standing there looking absolutely transfixed. Anyway, the moment passed and we said goodnight and I went in and shut the door and he went home. It wasn't until some time later that he actually wrote me a letter and in the letter he explained that he had been too embarrassed to say anything, but had seen an enormous glow of light surrounding me, orangey pink in colour. This he subsequently learned was an aura, and I found later that when working with stone circle energies it seemed to enhance one's aura. It happened again on other occasions but it was interesting that here was a very positive manifestation. We had a lot of other rum experiences too numerous to relate, including finding pre-flood images of a tortoise and other symbols, and a vast stone wheel high in the mountains.

After a while I left this part of Ireland, though I went back many times later. I drove slowly, wandering and wending my way across Ireland having adventures on the way.

It was odd that years later all the places where we had enjoyed picnics on the moors, and often the houses and hotels where I had stayed, were found to be meeting places of the IRA, or where arms were stored. Was this coincidence? I particularly wanted to look at some of the dolmens which are ordinarily called burial mounds and which are not burial mounds but initiation sites. These huge stone slabs supported by other upright slabs underneath have very peculiar energies, some very sinister indeed, situated over springs. In some places I had very unpleasant experiences. I was going over a peninsula called the Burren, looking at these dolmens, and the ground was composed of very strange hexagonal rocks with deep fissures in between in which grew really very rare flowers.

Dolmen

Some of these flowers were native to the Mediterranean and reputed to have been dropped there by birds when the waters of the great flood began to fall. They were quite different from any others elsewhere in the British Isles. It was a sunny afternoon and quite suddenly hail began to fall. I was really beaten to the ground and my camera was bashed. It was as if the elements were beating me off. I learned to respect this at a later date but I was suddenly afraid. I didn't know what I was afraid of except that no-one knew where I was or what I was doing, and I think I could easily like many people in past centuries have slipped down in between the rocks and lain there probably mummified in peat for ever. I stopped doing what I was doing and went home that day.

I went to find some of the holy places where some of the earliest Christians had begun teaching and preaching. How brave they were. Always their holy places and their hermitages were on sites where all the energy, or ley lines, converged. They certainly knew a great deal more about these than we do today. They also built their churches on these energy sites. One particular ruined cathedral in the west of Ireland I visited called Corcomroe was, like many others, built in the most wonderful place with very particular views. There are places in which one can feel out of this world, have miraculous feelings, as well as peace, beauty and utter, utter stillness.

We must strive to find these places within ourselves but when you are actually in them it is a very wonderful experience.

There is a lovely place in Ireland called the Dingle Peninsula, where heading out into the Atlantic is a very wild ridge of mountains with rocks and shores. There are reputed to be fairies there. I'm sure there are fairies. What are fairies? Little people only some of us can see. Anyway there are fairies on the Dingle. As I drove along I saw up on the hill some funny strange little beehive dwellings. These are the most ancient dwellings made by megalithic settlers who were the people who made the stone circles and initiation places – their dwellings were circular, coming to a pointed dome, quite small with a very low door. I left the car and walked up to them. This little settlement on the side of the hill had several beehive dwellings with all the doors facing inwards, and a very strange thing happened. It was a very windy day, so windy it was quite difficult to climb the hill to reach them. I entered the circle and sat by the door to one of the little beehives and there I went into a meditative and still state – an out of this world state – I sat down for quite a while, it could have been as long as three quarters of an hour. I imagined the little people who had lived in these dwellings and I just sat. When I came to and opened my eyes, I found that it was completely still inside the enclosure of the beehive dwellings, there was simply not any wind. The grass was quite upright and not bent over, but when I got up and stepped outside, the wind was just as hard as it had been before, blowing very strongly. There was something magic about this. Somewhere I came across a cell that was built by monks – the monks who inscribed wonderful, beautiful documents like the *Book of Kells*, in the finest brightest colours and gold leaf. Yet in these cells the only light was one tiny little square in the roof. I suppose they must have done it all by candlelight but the building was very remarkable in that it had stood all through these long hundreds and hundreds of years when things we know that have been built in the last eighty to one hundred years have collapsed.

On one occasion Paddy took me to visit a very famous writer friend who lived in an enormously high, square granite castle at the end of Galway Bay. Her husband was the single-handed yachtsman who crossed the Atlantic in his boat, Bill King. This was an amazing castle because if one climbed right up to the top and out on the roof, the whole of Galway Bay could be seen, as well as most of Ireland and out to the Atlantic – it was sensational. This was quite a visit and very Irish – we came down to dinner and the fire smoked so badly that we nearly had to lie on the floor. More and more things were placed over the mantelpiece, draped and propped, and everything else to stop it smoking, but obviously this was an age-old problem. We coughed and choked and managed to survive, but it certainly was very smoky. The company was very amusing and the table heavily laden with wonderful silver, not cleaned at all but very beautiful, in candlelight and we ate wonderful shellfish and the most gorgeous vegetables. We had to eat rather fast because it soon became very clear that the dogs and cats who also lived in the castle were allowed to get what they could when they could so one had to avoid giving them the chance as they got on the table to eat yours. It was a question of getting there first. Oh it was amusing and how we did laugh, truly memorable. The next day I told my hostess in the morning that I wished to go to Galway to buy some Irish sweaters for my small children. 'Oh, she said, 'We can easily do that,' so in her nightie, which was short, she jumped into her gumboots, pulled on two very large, long sweaters over them, popped a straw hat on her head and away we went to Galway. In Galway we drove up to what seemed a well-known sweater shop and I duly made my purchases and bought three marvellous jumpers for my

Galway Bay, Ireland

children. They were actually tied up in brown paper with string and the manager of the shop, who knew my hostess very well, saw her to the door, into her car and had a little boy who was also working in the shop hand over the brown paper parcel. Oh, what a joy that was. It took me back to the days when I was a child and my Granny took me with her chauffeur in her car to Selfridges in Oxford Street, stopping at the door to go and buy a paint box and brushes. Can you imagine – what a good life. Paddy and I were so badly bitten by fleas we decided to move on.

I felt that though there were people working for light in Ireland, my own work was in London. No-one can change other people. One can only try and add light to places where there is darkness, by healing and positive thinking in some way. So I went back to England, where I continued to dowse stone circles.

I went to Stonehenge several times, always with someone who understood that there are times, when involved in areas outside so-called reality, that one needs, like an electric charge does, to be earthed – the fact of having another well-earth being with me kept me from floating away into the ether.

Stonehenge is a very powerful place and must have been used for many reasons – I found the same lines of energy leading out from it to holy places as in other circles elsewhere. One warm sunny afternoon, I had been dowsing a while, trying to find answers about dates, energy types and other questions about stones, when it suddenly became quite dark and vast hailstones almost beat us to the ground. We became ice-cold and had to leave off. One of the guides told us that this had happened before when a party of dowsers had been there.

I visited other stone circles, one particularly forceful one at Avebury, but much has been published about this in other books. On the next visit to Ireland and Paddy, I travelled with Father Felix. Fr Felix was an Indian Catholic priest from Goa – a part of India where he said Christianity was still practised as taught two thousand years ago by St Thomas, who went there to teach. Felix had been sent to London to the Institute of Pastoral Studies on a three-year course which included psychotherapy and teaching about holistic medicine and healing. While there, he met my Irish friend Paddy and Felix and I were invited to stay at Rossmore. Felix was my ideal of a Christian priest, a youngish, very attractive person, with a great sense of humour, no inhibitions, and open to any information about anything. He learned some holistic therapies and practised them – he really was compassion personified. When we arrived at Paddy's house and Felix saw his room, he looked rather nervously out of the window and asked if there were pandas in the wood. It was like someone visiting from another planet, but nothing fazed Felix, and he was fascinated when asked to lay the kitchen table with the crested china plates. Felix and I went for long walks and had many meditations under the pine trees – a most healing experience for me, and where we could listen to the sound of creation. On returning home after one hard walk, Felix slightly shocked me by telling me to take my sweater off – and then gave me the most wonderful shoulder massage I've ever had. I was ashamed to have been shocked, and realised how conditioned and hidebound my thinking was! He did marvellous reflexology too. After some time he felt he would learn more in America, so he stayed with me in London then left, giving me his most treasured possession (he had no money), a book of meditation teachings by his teacher, Father di Mello. It touched my heart – the book is so precious and has enabled me to pass on much of Fr de Mello's teaching as practised by Felix. After training in America, Fr Felix returned to India where he set up a vast youth centre, firstly in Goa then in Bangalore, which are both very successful. Each Christmas we write to one another, and I'm always sent a new prayer. Here is one which was written by Father Giovanni in 1513 as a Christmas greeting:

> There is nothing I can give you which
> you have not; but there is much that,
> while I cannot give you, you can take.
> No Heaven can come to us unless our
> hearts rest in it today.
> Take Heaven.
>
> No peace lies in the future which is not
> hidden in this present instant.
> Take Peace.
>
> The gloom of the world is but a shadow;
> behind it yet within our reach is joy.
> Take joy.

If only there were more people like Fr Felix and Mother Theresa in the world. Mother Theresa spoke few words but said, when I met her in London, 'If everyone in the world thought for one second every day about love, the whole world's vibration would change.' I felt this could have happened years before, at the time of the Falklands war, and I had asked a clergyman involved in TV work if it was possible to find a slot for a minute each day on breakfast TV. The idea of everyone willing love on TV would be such a combined effort. The idea was rejected as impossible, i.e. it was not appealing to the mass media.

Later on in 1981 after one of my visits to Ireland and seeing some of the earliest Christian graves, abbeys and holy wells, I went to Scotland, to Iona, again to chase these wonderful healing energies. Iona is an experience, and like other holy sites it drew me like a magnet. I had the same strange feeling I have when I am getting near a stone circle or a special stone or well. The journey to the island was exciting by night train to Scotland, alighting in the early hours on to a tiny platform seemingly nowhere, into the freshest, cleanest air and the smell of heather all round and the hills, and silence. A small shelter with a mug of coffee and a wait, with a friendly porter, then on to Oban. Here we boarded the ferry to the island of Mull with its mountains, on to the bus, which took us across the island to another, smaller ferry. The sea by now was very rough, and sheep and crates and luggage and lots of local people were all getting wet, before arriving on Iona. I stayed in a hotel at the quayside – a long, whitewashed, reed thatched cottage, extended to become a hotel. I was with others here at a conference on reincarnation, but I wandered off – Iona in past history had belonged to the Duke of Argyll – a relation of my husband, Richard. But it had been given to the island with the abbey, as the Iona Trust.

The Iona community was formed and became a place where Christian worship was truly practised – communion in the wonderful old abbey really was a communion – the chalice was passed from person to person, so was the bread in a basket, so one really was serving one's neighbour. An early monk called Iona a thin island because there was only a thin layer between it and God. There were numerous beaches but the one I was most moved by was where St Columba landed on from his coracle when expelled from his beloved Ireland. He was told to go out to sea and only to land where he could no longer see Ireland. After what must have been a rough voyage, he landed on a sandy beach and the monk with him ran ahead and up the hill from where he shouted that nothing could be seen of Ireland. Later the island's fisherman told me that those who were favoured could find a special green stone on this beach – they are called St Columba's tears. It took me several visits at low tide to walk along the beach and search. I was favoured, and found three – a good omen – two I have passed on to other healers. The third I cherish. There were other beaches, some with mother-of-pearl shells and others where there were seals at play. We made a pilgrimage walking round the whole island and ending on the highest hill where there is a holy spring. The whole atmosphere and the light made it seem like another world. Talks and discussions about reincarnation brought up many subjects for thought, and people there spoke openly about their deepest feelings – much help was gained by all and a change occurred in many people's thinking. We made a trip to the island of Staffa where Mendelssohn wrote *Fingal's Cave*. It was a very strange island, with massive hexagonal rocks which looked as if they had been laid like crazy paving by a giant hand.

I returned to Iona again later – its magic unfailing, but so-called modern progress had crept in. The older islanders said it was a great sadness when cars weree allowed on Iona. Instead of stopping as on foot or bike to pass the time of day and exchange news, the cars just passed by – no contact, no communication – how sad that this lack of contact happens.

It can dry people up and make us more selfish – less giving, less able to receive – Christianity growing faint.

All this time, my healing clinic was in full swing. I was learning and reading and it again seemed as if each teaching or experience I underwent was given me just at the right time. Often if a patient had made an appointment any earlier I would not have known what to do, but I was ready, and it was a time of good synchronicity in my life.

Still filled with dreams of Iona, I returned to my home ground, Galloway in south west Scotland. It was here, in Whitehorn Bay, that the first Christian monk in Scotland, St Ninian, landed. The monks built a small chapel there and its views are of sand, waves and birds bathed in fantastic light. Gazing out I could easily imagine St Ninian meditating on this peaceful beauty. Like the cells of St Francis and St Columba, this building had been made with wisdom and an awareness of how contact with the natural world is as important for us as is contact with our inner self. I later came across a newly published, explosive book, *The Holy Blood and The Holy Grail.* This book proposed the possibility of a mortal resurrection after Christ's crucifixion, saying Jesus had married and had children whose descendants were alive today, and living in France. The story encompassed an enormous amount of historical information, and was a shocking theory but one which to me suddenly made sense of teachings I had always found unsatisfactory. It was thrilling. Much of the historical data was based in France (and Scotland), in places which I soon visited and I had an urge to know more.

CHAPTER FOURTEEN

Travel in France and Jamaica

Chastenay – Vézelay – Taizé – Jamaica

A<small>T THE END OF AN ENJOYABLE CAR JOURNEY</small> with friends across France, I came across Chastenay in Arcy-sur-Cure, Burgundy. Having

Chastenay, alchemical Château

toured many beautiful castles, churches and gardens, our last night was spent in Vézelay, a medieval town perched on a rocky hill. We drove up and up a winding road into cobbled streets that approached the town. Ahead, there was what looked like a coaching inn but was now a luxury hotel. My friends piled out to unpack before dinner but I felt my feet irresistibly drawn up the cobbled streets to the square above. I walked past many stone doorways, some with the Coquille St Jacques carved in stone, some with iron grills opening into dark little patios. On arrival at the top, at the end of the square stood this fantastic and majestic cathedral faintly pink from the setting sun, spires pointing high into the skies. Built in the middle ages, this cathedral is dedicated to Light and St Mary Magdalene. Inside, the impression really was of going into a very bright light. Tall pillars, some with black and white stone decorations, some adorned with extraordinary gargoyles and images, stretched along the length of the nave. This breathtaking sight did not overcome the tingling in my feet, and I was compelled to go along the side aisle to a small spiral staircase leading down to a dark, cave-like grotto. This was the rock on which were built the foundations of the cathedral. This grotto appeared to be a chapel, with dim candles lighting a grille at one end, behind which were some bone relics of St Mary Magdalene. The powerful feeling of holiness, energy, healing and all that St Mary Magdalene is to me was overwhelming, and I sat, outside time and place. This was the first of many visits to Vézelay and each time these feelings persisted. I felt St Mary Magdalene's healing energy directing me.

Vézelay had been the meeting place for those setting forth on the third crusade and from where the Knights Templar left for the Holy Land, and pilgrims to Santiago de Compostela. The experience of St Mary Magdalene led to many expeditions to places where she is supposed to have been, and one of these was Ste Marie de la Mer in the south of France, as I have told.

My friends and I set off the next morning, and there was talk of one more château as yet unvisited, and little known. Should we, they said, make a short detour *en route* to the ferry and visit? I said no, that we had seen so much, I had finished my camera film, packed up, and, as my Granny said, it's better to leave a party while it's still fun, so off we went. As we neared the turning to the château, my feet began tingling again and I admitted changing my mind, so my friends changed direction and made for the village of Arcy-sur-Cure and on to the Château de Chastenay. There it stood, an almost translucent place standing in deep weeds like the castle in the story of the sleeping princess. It was as if we were the Prince awakening the castle, and once awakened, what energies were unleashed. We parked the car and stepped out with a feeling that we had come to an empty uninhabited place, when out of the massive oak nail-studded door stepped a large, rather rough looking man in workman's corduroys and boots. He stepped through the magnificent archway lined with strange carvings and said in French, 'Ah, you've come to see my alchemical château of Chastenay, have you? I am Count Gabriel de la Varende.' We tried to explain that time was short and we didn't wish to disturb his work, just a quick look ... he walked on, disregarding all this and spoke.

The château had originally been built as a fortified manor in the eleventh century, within a walled enclosure. In the fourteenth century the manor was improved and had windows made where there had been slits for arrows. One of its inhabitants was an alchemist and had added a six-sided tower with a turret, and figures were carved on the windows; alchemical symbols. In the eighteenth century, a small, elegant drawing room wing was added. Chastenay was built on top of megalithic caves, which spanned three kilometres, and which had not been fully explored or documented, so this was a very ancient, historical place. The very special thing about Chastenay though was that it was built according to Pythagorean sacred geometry using methods passed on verbally from one generation to the next. Inside, the rooms were almost empty of furniture and seemed unlived in. Apparently it had been empty for years, and though it had always belonged to his family, Chastenay had passed back and forth to other relations and families, but now the Count had bought it back to restore it and live there. It soon became clear to me that Gabriel de la Varende was not simply telling the story of Chastenay in very rapid and voluble French, but that he was embarking on a great esoteric teaching of Pythagorean traditions, and symbols incorporated into the building, and what we were looking at was a message. The men who built this château used l'Art du Trait – symbols – keys to the science of the builders' sacred geometry which transformed the Pythagorean science of numbers into living proportions of a building. The master builders were continuing a work on earth which was begun in heaven by the architect of the universe. The shapes and decorations on the château represented the natural order of things.

On subsequent visits to the area I would feel the pull of Chastenay, and would always seem to arrive within view of the place if I was lost.

But my first visit there had to be curtailed and we left with a recently published book written by the Count as a present. I could not put this book down at home and wrote to the Count suggesting it be translated, and Jung's synchronicity being evident again, there was a letter that crossed mine in the post from the Count suggesting exactly the same thing. He wrote that it would have to be done by someone initiated into the teachings, who better than me. For three years I worked on the translation. My French was not good enough. I had to research words for medieval tools, from an architect, architectural terms; from a vintner, vintner's terms and so on, and finally every year from Count de Varende himself, translations from Burgundian local dialect. One year I took a small gite in a nearby village. I toured Burgundy seeing beautiful buildings – the Abbey of Fontenay, Bussy, Taizé, Cluny. I made friends with the village schoolteacher in Acey nearby, who took me on expeditions. We went to a huge restaurant which looked unhopeful, but as there were several rows of lorries parked outside, of course there was the best food and the most perfect wine.

Another time I stayed in Vézelay – able to visit the cathedral and grotto daily, particularly the chapel.

Most days I had some time with the Count – he was quite a strange person, sometimes cold and dark, hard to work with and yet always a teacher. Each day I learned more – he had immense knowledge and experience. His life had been as a Parisian lawyer, and during the war he spent many years in a Japanese POW camp and he changed, he said. Many people with a secure life do change after a traumatic experience, and break away from their conditioning and established ways of thinking. Gabriel de la Varende sought out his ancestral home, in ruins, and bought back Chastenay, devoting the rest of his life to its repair and continuation. People could come and learn esoteric knowledge through this beautiful building. For those who listened with their inner ears – the real pilgrims – there was much to be learned of esoteric law at Chastenay. The original builders had been men who lived with their families in the village for generations, and who if they did not already know were taught an age-old craft. They were housed on the estate, fed and paid, and they knew their work was not just work, but a positive creation for the beauty and glory of God. Such had been the builders of all the Gothic cathedrals. Later, it turned into palace building, showing the magnificence and wealth of people, no longer for the glory of God.

When I saw the Abbey de Fontenay I saw there the simplicity of St

Bernard who advocated minimum decoration, which he said distracted, but there were beautiful domed cloisters in which no doubt the monks paced and meditated. The only adornment I was struck by was a most beautiful wooden statue of the Virgin. I came away feeling St Bernard must have been so dedicated to the holy life that he was rather harsh.

Quite different was my visit to Cluny. It was one of the largest Gothic cathedrals in Europe, with immense columns, arched and fluted, and though a ruin now with only a small part remaining, looking upwards leaning against a column I could imagine the vastness of it and the beauty. Somehow the atmosphere was so strong it felt as if the place was still standing in all its greatness, and the powerful holiness emanating from this site could still be felt. It was quite hard to leave this place and get back to translating work at Chastenay, but each day the book progressed. History did not seem to relate many family stories until 1789 during the Revolution. The château and family survived the pillaging, so the story goes, because when the revolutionary mob came to attack they were entertained by the Chatelaine with such good Burgundy that they became totally drunk and the village folk managed to cart them away, so they left the château. Later, misfortune overtook the family and local people when the famous vineyards were wiped out by phylloxera and vintners were ruined. Maybe that was when the château was abandoned and fell into ruin.

Again, I took time off. I was literally spellbound by Chastenay – it filled my thoughts and held me in its grip. The earth energies were good and bad and very strong, and it is necessary to be vigilant in this sort of place, so one doesn't become overwhelmed. I got away for a while and visited Taizé. This was a place some miles from the ruins of the great Abbey of Cluny. A monk called Brother John had realised the need for all nationalities and all branches of Christianity to co-ordinate and become as one. He was joined by a few other like minds in a small hamlet called Taizé, where they founded an order based on integrated prayers and services mostly expressed in music, and they began to build a cathedral. After some years, this movement grew. There were so many young people in Europe searching for something different, yet within Christianity, and they began to gather at Taizé. This brave band of monks had really started something which was answering people's prayers. Taizé grew and grew, and so did the cathedral, which was pretty much completed when I arrived. There was a field of what looked like army huts – long tables and tents, and from the middle of this rose the cathedral. It was built of new brick and had the most amazing coloured glass windows. Once inside it was bare but for a few benches around the walls and some kneeling stools. There were millions of candles in gaps left in the walls. There was permanent music and singing. Sitting on the floor or kneeling on stools and joining in whatever was going on, was so welcoming. Services were alternately in French, German, Italian, Spanish and English – a lot of singing and guitar playing and music was kept up – wonderful tunes which have spread to many churches everywhere. I felt rather old as everyone seemed to be a young backpacker, but there was such an excited air at mealtimes and a good vibrant exchange of conversation that I came away singing. I believe the message of Taizé is now spreading far and wide.

Returning to England, I continued with my work, then I had a letter from Count de la Varende saying he had cancer of the liver, and asking me if I thought he should be operated on. My thoughts were that he should not, but I suggested he take massive doses of a herb I had been given from someone in America, for this purpose, called chapraal. This I believe has been imported since and extensively used. Besides the herb and other allopathic remedies, I said he should meditate in the alchemist's tower at Chastenay. I had a very clear picture of a meditation in the top of this six-sided tower drawing down powerful forces of light and energy to his body, which he should send down into the earth. The feeling of this healing and him going through the processes was strong, but I heard no more. The Count never answered a letter nor a telephone call. I presumed he was dead.

A year later, I needed to return to Chastenay to check a point in the book. I arrived at 6 p.m. when the count would be closing the château if he was there, and there he was.

He walked towards me looking better than I had ever seen him. 'A miracle,' he said, 'let us drink to it. I am cured.' We had some most beautiful white wine and then the keys were rattled and I was being dismissed. He was a strange person.

The translation was finished and back in London, as always when the time comes to move on to other interests, work was presented. I have since tried to get news of how the history of Chastenay continues, but it is strange that no-one yet has brought an answer – it is as though the whole adventure of Chastenay was a fairy story. Perhaps it was.

It was at a dinner party in London that I met a very interesting German with whom I found myself discussing colour. I was talking about Goethe's theory of colour and the Steiner course I had been on, from rather a mystical and aesthetic point of view, and he had apparently invented Dylon dye. He was from a well-known family living in their own palace in the eastern part of Germany until the beginning of Nazi occupation, when he and his family fled to England. Because he was German, he was interned in England for the duration of the war, so during this time he had time to think on his ideas. This was how Dylon dye was born. He had many business acquaintances all over the world, he had a lovely house in London and he was a very cultured person. We had lots of things in common. He invited me to stay with some Norwegian friends who had a house in Jamaica, so off we set together. We flew to Kingston, and the terrible truth was that our friendship as far as I was concerned had already begun to falter – I had felt he was a person of great strength on whom I might be able to rely as a partner for my older age, but it was not like that at all. We set off from Limeston Street, and as we stepped into the taxi all his travellers' cheques and everything else flew out and into the wind and he had to scrabble them all up so we nearly missed the plane. We then changed planes in Miami, and there it transpired that my travel agent had misled me, and I should have had a visa for America which I didn't have. I was shut in a cell, my passport was taken away and I had to wait for several hours while he went off – which rather annoyed me – and then I thought how awful it could be to be interned and shut up in a small space, as he had been, and I understood. We then spent a very hot day in Kingston hanging around in offices so I could get a visa and be sure of getting home. We eventually arrived at a most beautiful house near Victoria and I immediately felt that Jamaica was a place with good vibes, despite stories I had heard. The atmosphere was so friendly, and the people were so happy, always smiling and singing, and though they were obviously very poor, they were so nice. The house we stayed in was a bit sad because the Norwegians had transported all their own customs, and instead of having lush Jamaican food, we ate imported frozen fish and imported frozen vegetables, and cod-liver oil before breakfast. After a few days I managed to escape to the market, bought a basket and filled it with delicious exotic fruit. On leaving the market, I saw my hosts, standing outside absolutely demented and saying I was mad to go alone into the market, but I had found nothing but friendliness. I returned to the house and had to hide my basket of fruit in my bedroom cupboard where some went mouldy as there was so much of it.

Another day I met a well-known French artist who spent some of his time in New York and the rest of the year in a thatched house in a neighbouring Jamaican bay. He painted trompe l'oeil and had decorated a lot of the grand American houses in Jamaica. He took me one day to a settlement up in the Blue Mountains where the coffee comes from. There was a beautiful large Spanish house that had belonged to a slave overseer where a Jamaican doctor lived, who was practising exactly the vision that I had which was integrated medicine for everyone. This doctor had trained in Edinburgh, and then went on to Africa where he studied witch doctoring, learning about herbs and healing. He had installed his thirty-nine relations in this settlement and as they are slightly unreliable people he had given them each specific jobs. We went round and visited all these little departments. One was the herb garden; one of the plants, he declared, was the Tree of Life. Many years later, working with Dr Lambert Mount, we tried to get back and find this herb, but there was no reply to letters. Another department was the chickens, another the pigs, and another crafts in a large shed. Jamaican carpenters were making exact copies of Chippendale chairs, beautifully executed as they would have been when the British occupied in the eighteenth century. This amazing doctor and his assistant dealt with everyone there, and he could also use the hospital nearby.

I shall never forget the joy and bliss of swimming in the really warm sea of Jamaica, but it was rather sad, I felt, that we had to pay for the benches we were lying on, and for fruit drinks to be brought down by a butler wearing white gloves. It seemed to be making a mockery of something which had originally been so beautiful and untouched.

One day I walked alone to another bay where there was no-one except an enormous family of Jamaicans who were out with their children on a picnic. There followed the most interesting and entertaining time hearing about their lives. It was so simple and they seemed to appreciate all the nature they had around them all the time, and it was much more enjoyable than staying with the Norwegians.

CHAPTER FIFTEEN

Deeper Esoteric Understanding

Move to Chelsea – St James's, Donald Reeves and healing work – Knights Templar – Frédéric Lionel group – philosophy – Jung video – Selim – Beshara (Chisholme) – Ibn'Arabi – Morocco – move to Barnes – Uppark walled garden to attic – biofeedback – hurricane (Uppark) – Dr Lambert Mount

IT WAS A MIRACLE – the day I was to move into a smaller house in Chelsea, where I knew I could only have a small centre, Donald Reeves rang me to say he'd been offered the appointment as Rector of St James's, Piccadilly – and would I help with the healing part of his ministry? Here then, I thought, would be joy and space. He showed me round this beautiful large church and an equally large and beautiful rectory. He offered a choice of rooms for a healing centre but somehow it didn't happen. God's plans for us rarely do work out the way we choose. It seemed as if there was a restless grey cloud over each of the rooms in turn and in every corner of the church – unidentifiable but there. Perhaps because for so long a place used mostly for social occasions by birds of passage, the place had lost its roots. We had several healing services in the church led by healing clergy – but they weren't quite right. Then Donald had an inspiration. 'What about the tower up the spiral staircase?' he said. From that moment I knew deeply that this was right. But common sense began to prevail – how could the sick and lame climb up a spiral staircase in the cold and dark? But I knew something had to happen here. We went to the keys and Donald tried several which didn't work, but then my hand was drawn to one large key as I was saying, 'This will be the one,' and it was. A large old rusty key fitted the lock of this small heavy old door. Donald pushed it open and up we climbed – up a worn stone spiral stairway – the spiral we find everywhere in life spiralling up to the heavens. This one led to a huge attic space, with one glorious high window with small panes and the bell rope going through the floor. This

I knew was to be the place of healing and light. Donald understood and made it possible and I and a few loyal friends and healers set to to clear the cobwebs and dust and hauled up eight chairs; slowly it had begun. We lit the candle and three of us sat around it, this little candle which gave out a beautiful glow, pushing outwards into the darkness. We meditated on bringing the light to the tower, to St James's and to all who would work and heal there. We met one evening a week huddled in our thickest coats in the cold and dark with a lighted candle in the midst of our circle to meditate on light and inner warmth. The little group became a larger group, sometimes joined by others from distant places and the meditations were deep and very full of the feeling of spiritual light. It seemed as if we were clearing out the water at the bottom of the well so that it might spring up again clear and bright. There is a spring deep in the earth at St James's, and this was probably used for holy purposes long before even a Christian church was built there. The tower is the only original part of St James's Church that was not destroyed by bombs in the last war. This seemed significant, and we sent the light out in our prayers to many groups and people we knew which seemed to link us up with them. The light grew stronger and stronger while great things and activities were continuing in the church itself and in the rectory. Donald's ideas were taking shape and things were changing. There were those things and people from the past which were resistant to change, but change has to be accepted and that came about. The time came many months later when it appeared that those in the original meditation group were needed more elsewhere and healing was starting in a different form, open to many more in the church. Donald readily welcomed the idea of a permanent real light being lit in the tower to shine forth always so those who walk in darkness may be reminded of the light that is within them which is always there for those who seek. May the light always shine forth from St James's and grow stronger every day.

While the large curtains and carpets from the house in Argyll Road were just right for the rectory, I found the small house in Chelsea just right for me. My daughters all growing up and off to their own accommodation, and Harriet married, meant a different form of healing centre.

The healing changed its form too. No-one came many times as laying on of hands seemed to touch some deeper centre within some people as well as the physical, quite quickly. Many went on to learn more about healing for themselves and many came back even later to learn more and to know about dowsing and using the pendulum. It was good being next to St Stephen's Hospital. It was the right place.

Once I was established at Limeston Street, I found young doctors became interested in healing and used to come in their time off, not as doctors but as friends watching and experiencing in my clinic. Several of them got short term jobs at St Stephen's Hospital round the corner where it was convenient for them to pop in when they could. Many of them were absolutely horrified when they heard the accounts of patients and what had happened to them or what had not happened to them in hospital. Many of these young doctors broke down they were so horrified. The main omission always seemed to be compassion, understanding of a human being, a lack of time. They very much changed their attitude after they'd come to the healing clinic. Of course, they were healers themselves, and many of them started to use their hands. Some of them went on to special practices, private practices, where they found they were less inhibited in their ways; they needed to be free spirits. Several of them went to practise abroad. I'm still in contact with one now in New Zealand, where they find they can really practise their holistic medicine.

When I could, I got drawn further into the quest of the Templars, by a strange kind of magnetism, possibly the same energy that forms ley lines. I'd been to a lecture by Colin Bloy who started something called The Fountain Group. Colin had realised that a group of like-minded people working on the energies could change the atmosphere in a place, particularly working on ley-lines, which the Templars knew. I was over-awed when I looked at the screen because it was a map stretching right across the whole continent, and the places which were marked were places where I had been for no apparent reason. Some were very small and historically completely unknown so I realised there must be more to this than just a theory, so I was determined to pursue this further. I went to Scotland and one place I came across was a chapel built by Templars near Edinburgh called Rosslyn. Much has since been written about the Knights' treasure, even the Grail which could have been hidden there by the Templars when they were disbanded, and this has all been published, but it caused me to have many more visits to Vézelay and Chastenay in France and always back to Spain in pursuit of further Templar places.

In between visits to these holy places, I was continuing to study with Frédéric Lionel. A group had formed in my house and we availed ourselves of his teaching whenever he came from Paris, where he lived. Each meeting furthered our esoteric knowledge. He talked about the esoteric meaning of numbers, of architecture upon which the master builders based their Gothic cathedrals and had founded their work: cathedrals such as Chartres, Cluny, Léon. He talked about the original teaching in the Tarot, which came from middle Europe, and about the quest for the philosopher's stone, the unknown, white stone of knowledge. He taught the alchemy of self-transformation and he wrote and taught much else. Frédéric's teachings were of knowledge older than time, ancient wisdom known through all ages, an esoteric mystical teaching for all those who had ears to hear, but secret, therefore this teaching has been passed on by word of mouth so that it could not be destroyed. It passed on to Christianity and through the Knights Templar, and through the troubadours, who visited castles where some of the owners were able to teach their visitors. It was taught to pilgrims on their way to the crusades, at their resting places, to learn more of the meaning of life. I became more involved with my own quest for the meaning of life. In a way, I began to realise I had been irresistibly drawn to these places, like Newgrange in Ireland, Iona, Spain, Scotland, France and later Morocco and Turkey. All these were places where the Templars had been to teach and minister. Wherever they had been they left plants used in healing, many of which taught them by people in the Holy Land. Everywhere I found comfrey for broken bones, plantains for bleeding, both of which I always used.

At this stage I had to turn my thoughts to practicalities at home. Back in London, the more I heard Frédéric Lionel's teaching, the more I became aware of a different perspective of life and people. I knew then that I had to preserve his teaching in some form, I'd been shown a video of Jung talking, and I found it mind-blowing to actually see Jung. I had studied Jung and psychotherapy for some years with Ingareth van der Post, and also had an opportunity to meet the great man Laurens himself. The immense difference between hearing someone and seeing them, especially Jung, impressed me, so I thought Frédéric should be recorded on video. Little did I realise what I was in for – I could hardly work a video. A German friend who had made several videos of spiritual teachings and educational matters offered help. Frédéric wished to be filmed at his country house on the shores of Lake Geneva. He did not want to be filmed by anyone who did not understand his work, but it was hard and rare to find such a person so starting again with an open mind – not seeking, just letting things happen – someone appeared who did understand. I assembled a group of nine of Frédéric's followers, Polish, American, Hungarian, Swiss, British, German, and gathered them altogether in Switzerland, with the amateur video team and their van and kit. For three or four amazing days, we filmed, none of us really knowing exactly what we were about. The hardest part was keeping the peace over such occasions as meals in restaurants, transport – only the Americans and the Germans had cars, which they were unwilling to share – and other petty things. It made us realise how much more we had to learn and how very urgently Frédéric's message should be known and passed on.

A philosopher, sage and writer, Frédéric devoted his life to lecturing and writing, and has published many books. In our video, *Awakening to a Different Vision*, Frédéric spoke about chance being the law travelling *in cognito*, and related some war experiences to illustrate this lesson. He spoke about his master, Garcia, and he told us how our intuition could change our fate – destiny. Frédéric said the four master words were to dare, to cogitate (so as to understand), to will what is willed, to be silent. He also talked about overcoming fear, advising young people how to become Knights of the Spirit, and gave advice for healers too. He shared his wisdom, answered questions about world finance, the difference between power and authority and about punishment. Frédéric believed that only a revolution in consciousness would enable us to achieve a deep comprehension of the problems of our time, and dissipate the dark clouds on the horizon. He believed this was the birth of a new era, which would see a blending of scientific progress and a blending of eternal wisdom. It was only through a change of heart and consciousness that we could have hope for the future of civilisation in its true sense. For centuries, all spiritual teachers have called upon us to make this change. Frédéric said it was the task of the West to foster the emergence of pure humanism – not as a philosophical theory, but as an authentic expression of our innermost realisation. It is vital, he said, that we reclaim our destiny and strive to attain wholeness, so that fear may be replaced by hope and love by human endeavour. He quoted Hippocrates on healing:

The afflictions suffered by the body, the soul sees quite well with eyes shut.

Wise physicians, even among the ancients, were aware how beneficial to the blood it is to make slight frictions with the hands over the body. It is believed by many experienced doctors that the heat which comes out of the hand, on being applied to the sick, is highly salutary and suaging. The remedy has been found to be applicable to sudden as well as habitual pains, and various species of debility, being both renovating and strengthening in its effects. It has often appeared, while I have thus been soothing my patients, as if there were a singular property in my hands to pull and draw away from the affected parts aches and diverse impurities, by laying my hand upon the place, and by extending my fingers towards it. Thus it is known to some of the learned that health may be implanted in the sick by certain gestures, and by contact, as some diseases may be communicated from one to another.

It took some years to finalise the video and such details as the music. I particularly felt Scriabin's music was an appropriate introduction. He was an initiate and his music must have emanated much healing. After the Russian Ballet had been to parties in my house, they had sent me a live recording of the pianist Stanislav Richter playing Scriabin. I had heard him play at the Aldeburgh Music Festival, and can only describe it as heavenly, so it fitted perfectly into my plan – but to put all the master tapes together was another matter. No-one could be found with the technical knowledge and the understanding. But at this time I had the young Arab, who used to come for healing who I had housed because he was homeless, staying with me and said he would undertake the job, and enlisted what help he could. For days we sat gluing, cutting, whirring film to get things right – the music had to be fitted in to the introduction, most complicated. We laughed a great deal, and almost cried at times. But it eventually came together, and later on I got it professionally produced as two videos.

During the following years the Frédéric group made wonderful visits to holy places; once to Chartres where he taught and showed us the mystery of numbers and about sacred architecture, and about the reason for the great maze and the meaning of many of the symbols. We also went to Newgrange, Ireland, which was considered to be a burial ground, but by others an initiation site. This led into teachings about alchemy – these places where priests had undergone initiation by being entombed for a period of time where they went through an alchemical process of transformation. One of the key words to describe Frédéric was teacher, although he would not allow the word teacher to be applied to him. He was enabling transformation of the soul. One of my teachers was at the time the Arab boy who'd helped me put the film together. When he first came to me he appeared like an absolute dropout, but as time went on it became clear that not only did he understand Frédéric's teaching but he already knew it. It transpired his grandfather had been a Sufi, a tradition passed on through generations. Selim had been brought up in this tradition. As a child, his mother had escaped their home in Iraq with him and his siblings, at the time of the revolution. His father was killed and they had arrived in England as refugees. He had spent many years in Scotland at Chisholme with a group of Sufis, in a school of esoteric teaching Beshara founded by a Persian sheikh, Rauf Bulent. Selim passed on to me so much knowledge and deep spiritual understanding and practices. He had left Chisholme to wander and had somehow slipped downhill, having been deeply immersed in spiritual and mystical practices. It had affected him adversely, he became disconnected from reality. I respected his moments or days when he was strange, or even wandered off to sleep rough, but others didn't understand it. One sad day he was picked up by the police and got onto the treadmill of the social, medical network. He was locked up in a psychiatric hospital. It's well known that many monks and nuns in a state of deep meditation can go through the very thin line between sanity and insanity – a mystery not often dealt with because of a lack of understanding – and I think this is what might have happened to Selim. I visited him and always kept in touch whatever the state of affairs, and somehow we always managed to laugh. He had a great sense of humour. I've always found laughter to be the best medicine of all.

We got through many years together, several times in and out of hospital and through many happy times learning and practising together. It was so lovely to realise that Christianity and Islam, anyway Sufism, were, in the end, all one. Because of Selim I went to Scotland and found myself at Chisholme. It's strange that in life a certain note can keep repeating, like a coloured thread that appears and reappears from time to time, weaving on a loom until one is almost forced to pay attention. Many years before while working with Dr John Lester I heard him talk often about his life's commitment to the work of Gurdjieff. I had knowledge of this as a teenager as one of my mother's best friends had been the first man to translate Gurdjieff's work from Russian in the 1920s. John's whole life was immersed in this work, and other institutions linked to others, perhaps not quite so strict. This is what made me listen to Selim, and follow the present day thread of this knowledge at Chisholme. When I arrived there I wondered whatever I was in for. It was like being in another world, people from all over the world, all seekers of knowledge. I felt like a new arrival at school, but everyone seemed preoccupied with other thoughts – polite, but not chatty. One had to feel one's way into the organisation, and just observe and practise and join in what was going on. Every attention was paid to each action, the idea being that we are a reflection of God and therefore we must do everything we do to the very best of all our ability. Delicious food was beautifully cooked and presented for up to thirty people at each meal, there were flowers in my room and I was treated as a guest, not a pupil, so it was less harsh. Everyone was going about whatever they were doing, paying full attention to it all the time and time was spent in Sufi practice, in meditation and in physical prayer, and in a movement called Zikhr, which means remembering, or being reminded of, God at all times by a physical exercise. Part of the day was spent reading mystical works, principally of the Andalucian mystic, Ibn'Arabi. After taking it in turns reading there was space for discussion. Anyone could ask a question that had arisen in their mind during the reading which was examined and discussed. Time was allotted for thought, and reminders of God were given all the time, even when gardening, or building or cleaning or whatever the job. Every task was dedicated to God and had to be the very best. I was very impressed by this way of being and visited many times and each time came away with a fresh thought or feeling, having absorbed many different teachings, from the Koran, Christianity, the Gospel according to Thomas, the Apocrypha, Meister Ekhardt and more obscure writing. I learned that in the middle ages, there were, around the Mediterranean, schools of learning, where Jews, Arabs, Christians, holy men met to share their knowledge and practice. This must have been a time of great light in a dark world, when many threads of vast knowledge were passed on. Chisholme was not only spiritually refreshing and stimulating but I felt as if I were a child again, walking in the heather-clad hills, seeing deer and sheep and lochs full of trout, empty of responsibility and even much thought, endless mind space for imagination and intuition; even hearing the Scots language when I met local people gave me pleasure. There are still people and certain places unpolluted – it was as if I was ten, the same feeling I had at the holy well, drinking or washing in the water, or at a holy place with powerful earth energy. I was rather reluctant to leave always, but I carried away new thoughts to work on and explore and to share with others. So many people thirst for spiritual knowledge, but either don't know where to find it (we were told Seek and ye shall find) or are too fearful to ask – fear holds us back so often.

During these few weeks my healing centre was suspended so having returned from Scotland, and helped those who were waiting and who needed my help, I was off again, on a group travel to tour Morocco.

This was really as a result of studying at Chisholme and I wanted to follow Ibn'Arabi's tracks – to Africa again, undaunted by my sad visits to Rhodesia; this time my trip would be quite different. I had been inspired by my visits to Scotland and the works of Ibn'Arabi and this led me to Morocco, and later Istanbul and also I wanted to revisit southern Spain which I knew pretty well. The studies made me realise once again, if open to it, the oneness of things. Ibn'Arabi had participated in these schools, where initiated teachers of many religions met together to study this oneness. Some of the schools were in places I had been led to purely by instinct before I had even heard of Ibn'Arabi, places like Granada in Spain, and across to North Africa. As I queued in the airport in London a beautiful graceful lady, obviously Moroccan, asked my destination. Though I was joining a small group I had been slightly apprehensive travelling in an unknown country, without the language. I'd been told about the beggars, the thefts, the lack of transport or plans, hygiene, etc., so I was slightly nervous. This lady told me she was from Morocco and she said, 'You will love it and fall under its spell, but one thing you must remember is Walk Tall.' I understood well what she meant. The group was besieged everywhere by Moroccans clinging on to arms, clothes and even a handbag, offering help and guides and wanting to sell things. Those Americans, once they entered into conversation and started explaining why they did or didn't want help, were continually besieged wherever they went. I found, as advised, if I walked tall and simply remained unconcerned I was left in peace. Arabs have a most incredible sensitivity and underlying politeness which made them able to observe and sort people out – likely customers or a no-go area.

The first stop was Casablanca, with light and colours dazzling, sounds and smells all new and exciting, on to Rabat – what new vistas, such wonderful architecture, filigree work through which sunbeams shone at all angles, making a lace of sunlight wherever one looked. No buildings were adorned with carvings of fruit or animals, these are not allowed in Islam, but with the most delicate intricate sculptured stonework – no words can describe the breathtaking beauty. Colours everywhere, and clothes and drapes, fantastic bright saffron, oranges, reds and true blue, miles and miles of market stalls, an Aladdin's cave of gold, jewels, spices, sweetmeats, sheer beauty. The spices were not in covered pots but in open sacks, all the colours and smells blending into a most wonderful, heady mixture – how is it that some nationalities are so artistic? Maybe when we have less, we appreciate more. The poor in Morocco were very poor but they more than displayed what they had to the best advantage. Barbecuing meat in the streets with lots of mixed herbs, lentil and bean dishes, many kinds of rice coloured with saffron and sweet things too, so many varieties, beautiful clothes and leatherwork, which none of the group quite rightly were allowed to stop and buy. If we had it would have greatly detracted from our purpose of being there – it would have involved a lot of bargaining and we would not have been able to walk tall, or even move.

On to Fez, a city of dreams, the sights and sounds and smells will always be with me. I particularly noticed the graceful way in which Arabs walked, a quiet way, a way which looked as if they were very conscious of being, and were self-contained and centred. Was this, I wondered, as a result of Islam, having this permanent discipline, remembering God actively five times a day? We looked into a school, and small ragged children aged about seven were all learning the whole Koran by heart – reciting what they had learned, hour after hour – to start life with this feat is pretty remarkable. The narrow cobbled streets were so crowded you could hardly get a piece of paper between people. If a loaded donkey came by, at the cry of, 'Barak!', meaning, 'Take care!' all pressed even harder together to let the donkey pass. I felt it was so polite and courteous. We were taken to a tannery – the vast and evil-smelling vats of jewelled colours were quite overwhelming and the men working were dyed them-selves, probably internally as well as their skin, but the results were fantastic. I thought life here was cheap, though the results of the work done were beautiful. Fez was one of the places where Ibn'Arabi had studied, and though no guide today had heard of the great mystic, I saw the building – a mosque – where he had been. Everywhere ancient crafts were being practised still, rug making, weaving, dyeing, leatherwork, and all to the sound of copper being beaten into all shapes and sizes, for decoration and utensils, as it had been for thousands of years.

I saw too, watching these craftsman, how they enjoyed their work and what pride they had in their artistry. In fact job satisfaction, probably for a pittance. They had sun, it seemed, all the time, and though meagre food, it was good. They beat the copper and brass in a strange way, a particular and constant beat, and apparently this hammering is very special and is passed on through generations, to make special sounds to the glory of God, like a permanent chant. The vegetables in Morocco were the best I've eaten anywhere, and I discovered it's because the soil has a very high content of silicon. I had noticed that when we were going through the desert there were men lying buried in the sand with only their heads sticking out. It looked like a medieval torture, and people exclaimed in horror, but apparently this was to cure arthritis in the warm sand and silica which did the trick. We have on our own small island polluted all our sand and almost no natural minerals are left – how sad; it must be long past the time when everyone should have realised what we are doing, both to ourselves and to our land. We moved on until we were almost in the middle of nowhere, and we came across a Berber camp; a huge annual festival and horse fair. This seemed almost unreal. Fierce-looking Tuareg in blue turbans were in from the desert on their horses. These nomads were warriors and looked like hawks – they only came in from the desert on occasion. The vast Berber tents, very dark inside, spread over large spaces. Inside these tents, I noticed the floors were covered with rugs and sheepskin, warm and comfortable. The women, shrouded in brown and black kaftans, all sat together and cooked at one end while the men were waited on. It made me realise just what life as a nomad could be. No possessions at all, just the communal cooking utensils – I felt overloaded with material things. We all get drowned by them and forget our main purpose in life is to be, not to have. We only must have what we need, not what we want. The horses for sale were remarkable, Arabs of the finest kind – some looked noble and some looked scraggy – there were all sorts of fruit and vegetables of every description. This festival camp was clearly a great occasion to which country people had

come from great distances for an exchange of news and knowledge which was bound to happen, and also apparently, marriages were made.

So on we went through the Atlas mountains; it was so strange to travel from desert land and great heat to the mountains which were cool and where in the winter there was snow. Somewhere in the mountains we made a stop, near the holy city of Moulay Idris, only to gaze from afar as time was a factor. Moulay Idris was a holy city because it was the place where the saint was buried, and a place of pilgrimage. On we went and arrived finally in

Morocco

Marrakech. This was a city of fairy tales, men in the market selling every kind of food, spice and trinket and even water – most precious – from little brass bowls. Snake charmers were intriguing, and men doing the rope trick, apparently climbing a rope suspended in thin air – how the normal eye can be deceived. The bustle and noise and Arabic scents were heady. We were taken one evening down dark alleyways to a restaurant which had been a private palace. Food was served as it would have been to Moroccans – all sitting on cushions low down at round, ivory-inlaid tables. Huge steaming dishes of meats, rice, vegetables, were put in one earthenware dish in the middle of the table, and had we been Arabs we would have scooped it up with our right hands to eat. Tourists were given implements. Marvellous honey and nut sweets were followed by superb coffee. I returned home full of wonder and with some jewelled slippers and some rose petal jam. My impression was of a land of fierce strong people, colour, light, great art and mysticism.

Back in London again, a move from Chelsea to Barnes, I realised later that this was just before the time of the fire at Uppark. Feeling restless, it was time to move my tent again. I had missed my garden at Uppark. I'd given my magic cottage in the walled garden to Sophie when she married, and confined myself to the attic in the house at Uppark. I was very much in touch with the grandchildren, but it was sad to look down on the garden (not mine) from so high up and not be able to run out and get my hands in the earth and into my herbs every day. I realise I have all my life needed to be near earth as though it were oxygen, to revitalise myself. Equally, at one time, I and other healers working with me found we seemed to be overcharged with electricity – I would get a severe shock when I touched keys, the cars, the button in a lift, and so on. This could be remedied by putting one's hands flat down on the ground, as though to get earthed. It is a curious experience, showing the energy as both positive and negative.

I felt very restricted and trapped at Uppark – all those stairs, doors and what seemed like miles of corridors to get out. There was change all round, and my little house in London, next to the Marsden Hospital which had seen so much healing work, seemed to have come to an end. I remarked to a friend that I'd like a house in London where there was a village green and a pond, with a garden, and there it was, just what I wanted waiting for me in Barnes. There was a lot of healing work too at this time, groups of therapists were coming together to exchange views and experiences. I remember on a trip through France coming to a small town and a tiny church containing Jean Cocteau's grave; there he had painted herbs and healing plants up the walls. He knew all about healing herbs and homeopathy and was an initiate. His simple gravestone was in the centre of the chapel, and as I looked, a wonderful jewelled light, red, blue and yellow, shone down on it from the window, and the stone read: I am always with you. It was very moving. Jean Cocteau had surely been on the path of initiation. I met yet another nice doctor at the right time too, and it was a very valuable experience to work with a doctor who was very open to new experiences rather than the confirmed orthodox approach – these were fearless doctors, with time for compassion and listening. I attended many workshops and lectures on complementary therapies but they were for me only tools if required. I had my hands which I had been given to use – it became more exciting as doctors and healers openly began to work and meet together and now things are becoming even more integrated as people lose their fear of the unknown – not really unknown, but lost in the speed of progress. Wise old men and women in mountains and by the sea in so-called unsophisticated parts of the world all know these things and have practised healing since time began.

As usual Uppark drew me back, and much had been happening there meanwhile – I now had seven grandchildren, the last arriving in 1989. They are an enormous joy. I like to give each one completely individual attention, so important, and I like to have time to think out answers to questions, properly – some of the really important moments in my life have been listening to the answer given to my question from a real teacher. It amazes me how true and straight a child's question is, and I find I have to be more and more soul-searching to find proper answers. Why are we here? No child asked this, but when an adult does, I feel it is a huge step on their journey.

Though enjoying being with the family, especially the eldest lot who lived in the big house with me, and other young people who came and went, it was time I moved away a bit. I needed to stand back and try not to breathe down their necks. Having suffered so badly from this myself, from my own parents-in-law, I was determined not to repeat history. When my daughters came with various boyfriends it was very difficult not to judge. This I know is wrong – how dare a parent set a standard for the next generation, yet there must be some line of demarcation. I remember a conversation with Hephzibah Menuhin, who was a good friend. She said one should not bring children up with a specific religion – one should offer ideas and help them explore. I on the contrary maintained one should teach them the basics (in my case Christianity) of parental religion, always with the proviso that if they found something which was better for them they should pursue it. I felt a child needs a yardstick with which to measure, who knows? Through the years I had many close boyfriends, but never married again for various reasons, but one major reason was that I could only have lived with someone who had a free spirit and with whom one could communicate at soul level, completely honestly. I did have two such friends at different times, but I also had to weigh up my family at Uppark against someone else's equally important surroundings. While I was in the attic, one small grandson, aged about six, used to come all the very long way up, with his pillow, to share my bed very early in the morning. He had to make a huge journey up two flights of big stairs, and through three very heavy doors, but he braved it. I have noticed this closeness creates an important bond which seems lacking in those children with whom I didn't share this special time. I feel so many people have become out of touch, and a great part of healing is the human contact, the human touch. Like switching on a plug. Years before when I was studying biofeedback with instruments that registered the brainwaves and their behaviour, it was observed that though the brainwaves of a sick person and a healer would register a quite different state of mind at first, after a while both brainwaves would be the same. I noticed too when I was doing meals on wheels that people were more starved of touch almost than food. They responded to a healing hand almost as if they were thirsty and were being given a drink. On a spiritual level, we read in many teachings that people were told to go to a well and drink, meaning spiritual water. Those who were thirsty were given a drink of water – spiritual assuagement. All around us nowadays we have those who are thirsty to whom, if we know how, we can give a drink. I was so fortunate to be near my family as we all shared this view. Here were all the family living within walking distance of each other, yet having quite independent lives. Harriet and John with Charlie, Maria and Edward; Emma and Geoffrey with Oliver, Harry and Matilda; Sophie and Angus with Theodora.

But at this time there came a change at Uppark in the house – shutters clanged shut at six, winter or summer, even on a bright, sunny evening. Lights were turned off, all the furniture out of season instead of looking beautiful and asleep like Sleeping Beauty's Palace, was zipped into white clinical covers and stacked, which made the house look not asleep but dead, except for the life going on upstairs; then came a sort of warning – a hurricane. One terrible weekend in 1987, when luckily none of the family were at Uppark, there was a devastating hurricane. It swept in from the Isle of Wight. Uppark was in the eye of the storm, at six hundred feet high. Many avenues of trees two hundred years old looked as if a giant hand had swept over them, bashing down and uprooting all the big beech trees – beech trees have shallow roots – and the dreadful sight of two-hundred-year-old trees upended with their roots in the air and all the earth still on them crashed on the ground seemed almost surreal. Many of the surrounding trees were crushed down under them and lying like wrecks all round. None fell on the house, thank Goodness. The first sign of life on this terrible morning was a call from the National Trust curator to ask if someone would remove the enormous tree fallen over the drive as he and his wife must get away on their holiday to Spain! There were no alarms in the house, the house open to the wind. Rapidly the family rallied and came from wherever they were. They immediately set about putting to rights communication and access to the house. There was no electricity nor telephone so things had to be salvaged from vast freezers, burglar alarms had to be put right, all the various modern equipment relying on the services had to be dealt with. And far worse was the future of all these trees – many years clearing and replanting had to take place. This in itself was in a way a challenge to keep going and replant the trees on an estate which had been nurtured at various times depending on the family's financial situation and had to be carried on as a continuity of history – a history of place and family of hundreds of years. Had we known it this seemed a kind of warning, a premonition. It was a dreadful shock to the family, and even the air of the place had a curious electrical discharge in it, not pleasant. But worse was to come, not water, nor wind, but fire.

At the same time as the hurricane was happening at Uppark, a tragedy had occurred in London. Brilliant and beloved Dr Lambert Mount, with whom I had shared such exciting work, was dead, murdered by a patient. I felt so strongly at the time that he was needed more elsewhere, in another realm. It seemed as if he had been tuned in to a much holier and higher vibration than our coarse one here. He had been a follower of Subud, and he was a deeply spiritual person.

Wonderful things were happening at the healing centre – one woman with terminal cancer and a medical estimate of only weeks to live asked if she should go to South Africa to see her parents – my feeling is that one should die doing what one loves doing. So my answer to her was to go – this was against medical advice, but so what? I heard no more and presumed she had died *en route* to South Africa or while there. About a year later driving down my road I had to brake for a woman crossing the road, and I recognised her as my patient. It was pointless to follow up what seemed like a miracle – either it happened or it didn't – and I was happy to see she was alive. Another woman came to see me in the same state, an Irish girl. I first went to her in hospital, from where she got slightly better. She came for healing and I knew without her telling me that she was terribly homesick – too ill to travel. I could hardly believe my ears when I found she was from the remote village in Ireland where I had done so much dowsing in stone circles and places of healing. I suggested she went home against all odds – that she went and found the village carpenter, who I had taught to dowse and heal with his powerful healing hands, and ask his help. I told her to go and sit in the very little known stone circle where we had worked and I knew she would receive healing. Whether she died or lived was in God's hands, no-one else's, and healing happens in all dimensions. Again I heard no more. End of story. Two years later she arrived on my doorstep in London with a huge bunch of white lilies. She was completely well and had done all I had suggested, and had sat in the stone circle and had met the healer. She was working for a religious institution teaching meditation and was so happy – the miracle had happened. The curious thing too was that the lilies, bought and given with so much love, lasted an awesome length of time, many weeks. Flowers also tune in to what is happening. This was a time too when Selim and I were trying to put together the video of Frédéric Lionel. As always, I listened to Frédéric Lionel's wisdom and went to his meetings, and struggled to put together the videos I had produced. His teaching incorporated much else that I was learning and reading about. One thing was the history of the Knights Templar, that I had touched on, seeing their vast fortresses when I was travelling in Rhodes, Malta, Spain and Scotland. It was almost like a personal search for the Holy Grail. Rosslyn chapel in Scotland, the possible treasure trove, was a most strange place, carved with foreign fruits and bizarre symbols in stone. These have since been researched and written about and prove the people who carved them must have been to America where the fruits and flowers grew at a time before Columbus.

CHAPTER SIXTEEN

Tragedy at Uppark

Uppark fire – Heveningham – Al Ghazzi – Spear of Destiny – *Book of Kells* – Koran – Spain – Turkey

Back at Uppark, one weekend in August 1989, a crack had been found in the ceiling of the saloon. The family had given their home to the National Trust, in trust, and this, with nature and the hurricane, was to have a terrible consequence: real trouble began. The house was invaded by workmen, seemingly without regard for the life in it nor its contents. Every part of the building was disturbed, dry rot and death-watch beetle were discovered which most houses of this date would divulge if laid bare. Everywhere things were moved, shoved around, the roof had to be repaired, it became bedlam. The family persevered and bore with it with good will and courage and much hard work, trying to cherish the beautiful contents the best they could, but now life was disrupted and it was disturbed. It was a most unhappy time – there seemed to be restlessness in the air. Each week I returned to London where the healing centre helped me keep my inner calm, not easily, but it was a peaceful and still place where I could focus and rearrange my energies.

It had been while I was living in the attic, that I had felt the whole atmosphere darken. I knew that something awful would happen. I repeatedly warned that the way the workmen were working would be the cause of some trouble; but no-one would listen. People in remote National Trust offices disregarded my warnings. They didn't live there and they didn't feel the darkening atmosphere; they didn't see the weekly work amongst the rubbish going on on the roof outside my dormer windows.

And then, in 1989, I started to hear Sarah's voice, and she said quite clearly one day, 'They are destroying it.' The voice went on and on. 'They are destroying it, they are destroying it.' It got so bad I heard myself repeating it out loud. I thought I must be going mad. I went away, I went up to London – and that day it happened.

In three hours, all the magic, love, craftsmanship, work, generations of cherishing was gone – FIRE.

Fire, the most violent of nature's elements, burned Uppark down. I was in London, settling in to a tiny flat when a call came from Emma. 'Mum there is a terrible fire at Uppark.' How I drove there is a miracle – I arrived to see huge hoses and fire engines all up the hill and in the drive – and there from the entrance gates I saw a sight that caused one of those out-of-body times, when there simply is no feeling, as it is all too remote from reality. It was like witnessing, from some remote, disconnected area, a James Bond film: beautiful Uppark blazing, flames leaping up into the sky, flames leaping out of all the windows and doors, and then, after regaining my breath, reality hit. There were firemen and people everywhere. My family, who had been in the walled garden, had rushed along organising a chain of people to salvage furnishing and anything from downstairs that was removable. They did amazing work.

As I stood there I remembered cases of precious things that were in the basement safe. I seized a fireman, who told me that he could still get down there if someone showed him the where. The cases were saved, but that was all, out of everything we possessed.

Nothing had been saved from our upstairs flat, not one thing. I heard afterwards – I still do not know if it is true – that the National Trust have a rule in case of fire: to save their own things first. These items were on the ground floor, so those were saved, although the fire had started at the top of the house.

The family were magnificent in their organising, and even under dire circumstances kept their heads and did exactly what needed to be done. I was completely shattered, devastated; there was my life's work – and it had been very hard work on my own – gone in three hours.

The flammable roofing material burned, as one would expect, all the windows were open, and it was hot and dry. The house burned like a haystack.

A photographer had been with the public taking a photograph, and saw smoke rising in the roof. She alerted the crowd. It seemed ages before the fire brigade finally arrived, the fire by then raging. Then it was discovered there was no water. The water tanks were empty. The swimming pool was useless, the village was six hundred feet below. There simply was not enough water anywhere.

One of the worst parts then were the public and the media, who were like crows around a dead corpse. Helicopters circling overhead, photographers everywhere, photographing the family in their grief. One camera lens zoomed up to my face and in a rage I struck both camera and photographer asking how dare he be so intrusive. 'And anyway,' I said, 'where do people like you come from?' Later, he only published a long-distance photograph of the family. What hurt me during this time was some people's insensitivity – crowds and crowds of people behaving like ghouls – what is it in people that makes them enjoy a spectacle at a time of tragedy and ruin and total destruction of something beautiful – what goes through their minds at such times?

The Trust did not act as if they were interested in the families that live in their houses, though the houses would not have existed without them, nor indeed would the National Trust. One of their directors suggested at a meeting that the family might like to live elsewhere: that would have been convenient for them.

News of the fire was international. The media never mentioned the family directly, but I still received calls from Europe, America, even Australia, to see if we were alright – mercifully we were because none of us had actually been in the house. Then the lawyers moved in. A most distressing time followed, on and on it went.

I felt that this was the end of a long sequence of events where the original aims and wishes of the National Trust had been allowed to be undermined and diluted. It appeared to us that the first Trust representatives had understood the whole way of life that went on in an ancestral home. They were critical, but constructive and humorous. James Lees Milne was one of the original trustees, and in his book describes most outspokenly some of the owners on his visits – he was really rude and critical, but people who knew him did not mind. It was done with grace and humour and he had manners. Slowly all this disappeared. As it grew in size and perhaps in self-importance, the National Trust became a faceless body, no-one taking personal nor individual responsibility.

After the fire there was a lot to do from the family point of view. The family were the losers, not only of all our priceless heirlooms and all our personal possessions and home, but as far as media were concerned, we did not exist.

However, from the ashes rose three powerful phoenixes: my three daughters, with their husbands and their children. They were marvellous about the fire. Their home destroyed, they soon made another. They were an example noted by many of real family teamwork and have been ever since. I believe the most important element of a country is proper family life with a shared belief in compassion, work and enjoyment. This also incorporates responsibility, faith in one's own work, proper communication and manners. A family with these sorts of unwritten rules can survive most good things and bad, within their own orbit, drawing strength from each other and support. Repair and work went on and on for eleven years, and many young craftsmen executed wonderful restoration work. It was good that this work was not only beautiful, but it gave many of these young men a wonderful chance to work and set out well-equipped and experienced on their own journey in their own craft.

At this time I had an Arab friend, an oil rich Bedouin who had bought one of England's most beautiful houses – Heveningham in Suffolk – decorated by Wyatt in the eighteenth century. It had fallen into disrepair. Restoration was lavished on it, and he used it for many large weekend parties. The interior of the house had been refurbished with beautiful painted walls, gold decoration, marble floors and so on, but it had been furnished only sparsely and he hired tables and chairs for parties. The best chef and helpers in London came, a well-known orchestra was hired and great music was played on the occasions on which he occupied it. The bedrooms were furnished only with a bed and bedding of the greatest comfort, wonderful rugs, bathrooms with gold fittings and nothing else. There were also bowls of exotic fruit and lots of flowers. This charming, kind Arab had such interesting parties which were a great distraction for me. Politicians from all over the world, world-wide bankers, businessmen, some grand county neighbours and others including diplomats stayed for weekends.

Amongst the people I met here was an Arab scholar with whom I had interesting religious discussions. He told me a great deal about calligraphy and the different illustrations in the Koran. He told me we have the best Korans in the world in the British Museum, so later I spent many days looking at these absolutely fabulous books. They are quite different from European books, and are illustrated without animals or flowers, but with symbols and signs that look like filigree work, and these all have significance, intimating passages from the Koran and in praise of Allah. While I was doing this I know I was in touch with the infinite. Being in contact with these decorations was in fact like a yoga because it is in the act of looking at them combined with a state of meditation, which has a very deep, more than visual effect.

While in Vienna in 1961, I went to visit the Hoffberg Museum and saw many treasures there. As I was walking along, I was drawn like a magnet to a case which had armour in it and a spear. Normally these are the things I am not interested in and would have passed by. I really was drawn by the spear in this case. It was on red velvet and the label said 'The Spear of Longinus'. Well, I didn't know anything about the spear, I didn't know why but it simply held me in a sort of magnetic grip, and I came away feeling that some sort of power had been added to my dimension. I completely forgot this, and a great deal more happened, until much later when I heard about the Spear of Longinus. Known as the Spear of Destiny, reputed to have been the spear that a Roman soldier used to pierce the side of Christ on the cross. The saying was that whoever had it had power over all else – a power over his destiny; and the spear passed through many hands over time and was kept in the Austrian empire for hundreds of years. When World War II was being fought, Hitler was very much into the occult and very much counted on occult talismans and signs and secrets and was guided by them, and he must have known about the Spear of Destiny. The Nazis got hold of it and it disappeared. There were many stories about it. At one time the SS took it to Poland where they hid it and then they moved it and eventually, when the Nazis lost the war, the Americans were sorting out the national treasures and regalia (to be returned to the countries they belonged to) and nothing was mentioned of the spear until General Patten spoke up. General Patten was very knowledgeable about esoteric and occult things and he knew the real meaning about the Spear of Longinus. He tracked it down and through many vicissitudes saved it, and eventually returned it to Vienna where it is now in the Hofberg Museum. It is strange that this magnetic thread wove its way into my life without me knowing what it was about.

But I later tied it up with one or two other occasions when I was with psychically powerful things, the means by which through the object's emanation I seemed to detach from material things and be in a place where there is no time and no space, in fact putting me in touch with the infinite. One instance was in the 1970s on my visits to Dublin. I went to study the *Book of Kells*. The *Book of Kells* is one of the oldest known illustrated manuscripts, written and painted and put together by monks. There was an exact replica made many years ago in Switzerland, that with permission one is allowed to handle. I sat with the *Book of Kells* in the museum for three days, just studying each illustration and page, turning over pages as I absorbed them. These pages had sometimes taken a lifetime to put together in the most wonderful colours and gold leaf, and the letters were entwined with the very oldest Celtic symbols, all of which mean something, and with strange birds and beasts and fantastically beautiful flowers; a real wonder to behold. Here again I was completely out of time and space. I had no idea what time or day or place it was. It took quite a while to get myself back and my feet on real ground into real time, and this was the same feeling as I'd had looking at the Spear of Destiny all those years ago in Vienna, and studying the Koran in the British Museum. I feel sure this is what was intended by the creation of these magical works, contemplated by monks and mystics through the ages. This yoga connected them with the divine.

I was so grateful to my friend, Al Ghazzi, for introducing me to many people with great minds with whom I could have a deep discussion about philosophy and religion, as well as more casual things. It took me a while to realise that, in true Arab fashion, his whole family worked for him. One brother was the chauffeur, one the chef, one carried up the luggage and others did various other jobs, and one was in the business. They all seemed so happy. My friend afterwards paid me the greatest compliment, when my last and seventh grandchild arrived, he said, 'Now you really are a tribe.' He was right. We really were and are still. He did come and visit us at Uppark, and I think was amused and bemused. Sadly, he died young and the house was sold and the family dispersed.

While Uppark restoration went on, I settled into my new house in Barnes, the house near a village green with a pond, making yet another garden, which was my obsession, and doing much healing work. Further editing of the video I had made with Frédéric Lionel was proving very hard work, but it was finalised here, and I was able to show it to certain people. Very few people are able to break out of their mould – many live on a track they dare not get off – fear is the worst enemy of all – yet those who make the quantum leap both physically and in their thinking become free. Free to be themselves, to find what they really are, what they really can do and what they really believe. Those who dare to change are those who really live life to its full potential, and miracles do happen – a miracle is only that which is beyond the normal comprehension of man – once we are truly free we can tune in to the rhythm of the universe, into the cosmos, which means 'order'. Many young people now are doing this. I think the pressure of the normal track of life is becoming too hard and fast to be sustained – it is only when we hit rock bottom, and are confronted with a situation of illness or tragedy we cannot deal with, that we have to look at things we normally would not have seen. We would have passed by – it is then that we wake up.

It is interesting to note that all these years while people's thinking is changing, in their lives, so also is science. No longer is Newtonian theory accepted, but there is an element of probability rather than certainty – quantum physics is taking foremost place. New physics and technology is enabling us to discover that much more was known in all ancient sciences, including astrology, than we in the present civilisation know now. Things are being found now which were known thousands of years ago. All these thoughts provoked much fruitful discussion in places like Barnes!

I made further short travels, and when I reviewed the travels I had made before, I could see a pattern of discovery – as always a worldly discovery leading to a spiritual discovery – I had been drawn all those many years ago to Egypt, where the oldest civilisation began, and to the knowledge of Pythagoras which in conjunction with the Pyramids was built as a reflection of the stars. In Mexico I saw the same Pyramids, where the crystal skull was found and where the seat of knowledge of the Mayans was and where a calendar of times and days had begun.

This led me later to places in Europe – as always Spain, where I went every year, discovering the places where the Muslims had overcome the Christians. Many years earlier I had visited Spain and starting in Madrid I went south to explore places starting with Granada and the Alhambra Palace, but most impressively the Generalife Gardens. These were gardens built by the Moors, who had realised the best possible use of water. There were paths and courtyards where the water had been arranged so as to be a permanent music and where you could sit and contemplate and meditate to the sound of water, and the sight of it flowing through wonderful marble fountains. One could walk and smell and sit among the orange and lemon blossom and lilies and lavender and herbs. The Moors realised the effects these things had on people returning from war and strife and they appreciated the beautiful things that were already in this country. I looked more careful and fully into Islam, at the way they decorated their palaces, showing sunlight. After Granada we went on to Malaga and to other places.

In Cordoba, we visited the Mesquità, a wonderul Moorish mosque containing in its very heart a vast, elaborately decorated Baroque cathedral. It was rather strange as it had domed ceilings with seemingly endless columns of black and white marble. While we were in Cordoba there was a special festival for La Macarena, the virgin of the toreadors, who is reputed to cry. She was brought out on her throne and processed round the streets for all to be blessed by her and admire and see her. Another day it happened that Franco was visiting, and the streets were lined not with people in festive mood, but with the army, and Franco was driven past in an armoured vehicle, standing up. I was very surprised because he was very short and stocky, but he looked a very strong person, which was interesting to have seen. We went on to Seville, full of beautiful things, and we also called in to Jerez, the seat of sherry, and were shown round by the Gonzalez family who have run it for very many generations. It was an enjoyable distraction at the end of rather a serious tour. But the interest in the religious part of it to me remained in my mind and I wanted to tie it up with more exploration. Before this particular trip to Spain, I had many trips to Scotland and to Ireland where Christianity had begun, and where ancient religions had been incorporated into Christianity. The Knights Templar had brought much learning back from the crusades: mathematics, geometry, astronomy, alchemy and medicine – in all these gathering places an inner teaching was given that was passed to the freemasons. The teachings became underground because of perse-cution, but it was interesting that once I got on the trail they could be found again, through exploration, reading and thinking. All these threads of knowledge in my life came and reappeared, but I was always able to maintain healing for others. The doctors who came into the healing centres at various times were experiencing the same sort of shift. We were all pilgrims on the journey. In all my experiences, I had felt in a very small way, what those mystics must have shared in the great places of learning all over the planet. The holy essence or atmosphere can be felt in places where spiritual practices take place and are kept alive, in the many places I have described, and also to a certain extent in Greece, especially on Patmos where St John had his Revelations – almost always in places where there had been monasteries and people had lived out their beliefs.

It was these places which inspired a trip to Turkey. Istanbul was a revelation. It was unlike the feeling I had flying over the North Pole and Newfoundland to America, when I had felt like a grain of sand before the vastness of the land, sea and mountains, where it looked as if God had poured it all out of a bag; earthy, tangible. Flying to the Middle East was not like that at all, but like the opening of a tunnel into a new world atmosphere; the east with all its horrors and romance, with thoughts of Genghis Khan and his hordes sweeping onwards over the mighty Ottoman empire, of the forces of Islam and Christianity, of which pockets still remain there. Then came the thrill of actually standing on the balcony of the

Topkapi Palace, Istanbul, still in Europe, looking out on to Asia across the Black Sea. The west and east joined here. All those hundreds of cultures suddenly realised as one – somehow the whole flavour of Istanbul brought home to me the stories of the *Arabian Nights*; the caskets of jewels on display in the palace. I was actually seeing gold boxes encrusted with every gem ever worked; rows of pearls, cups made of gold. The architecture was such a joy to behold – every window and door in palaces and mosques decorated with filigree again all designed in the secret, sacred patterns, and expressing and praising the name of Allah. The sun filtered through the windows like golden threads. All I saw was as much a spiritual experience as a physical one. I visited the tomb of a Sufi saint on the shores of the Bosphorus, which was quite an adventure. He was called Azez Nahmud Hudaji Effendi. I left the group and into a taxi I got, with just a piece of paper with the saint's name on it, and no address. The taxi driver, with the enthusiasm I met with everywhere in Turkey, set off. Up, up we went, higher and higher through a myriad of streets that got narrower and narrower, with frequent stops and endless conversation and pointing. Eventually, we went up a cobbled street, really only for pedestrians, at the end of which we had to stop as we were wedged between walls. With much excitement at the realisation of what had happened, we were pushed back by a crowd now gathered round us to try elsewhere and then we reversed. At last the tomb was located, and I found myself being watched. The driver very sensibly indicated to put my scarf on my head, and I went into a courtyard to see the tomb behind a grill. Having made my obeisance, I was accosted by some young students who spoke French. We had an interesting conversation as to why I had come. Because, I said, I had studied with Sufis and admired the Koran, but when asked directly if I was a Christian, which I said I was, they all turned their backs and walked away.

Our group stayed in a hotel which had been a Turkish house – curious rooms with lattice windows all opening onto a courtyard in the centre – this place was rather quiet and secretive. So many of the narrow streets seemed like this with no women about. Then the thrill of going down the Bosphorus on a boat seeing the curious wooden houses on each side; the excitement of the souks; streets and streets of beautifully arranged goods, in many colours, enticing edibles smelling fabulous – some streets of gold jewellery, some of slippers and fabrics . . . then I noticed the terrible poverty too, beggars with no legs and terrible sores and one wondered how these injuries had come about. Maybe it was the result of disease, and I realised there was no free medicine or handouts or free rights here, but even so the crowd in general seemed made up of so much happier people than in England. There were many streets of restaurants too, but my main impression was of the mosques. On entering any mosque I had such a very powerful feeling of the constantly energised holy spirit in a place where holiness is practised continuously. The feeling of prayer seemed to swirl and rise as one's eyes looked upward to beautiful domes, which increased in volume as they got higher, somehow expanding in praise. In a Christian church when we look upward it narrows into a point and a spire. It felt so welcoming to walk into a mosque, remove one's shoes and pray on the most fabulous carpets and rugs. I noticed many acts of respect shown, which we in the west seem to have forgotten or stopped. Washing feet and hands before entering to pray in a hot dusty land made people more aware of what they were doing and why, and who in the west remembers God five times a day, publicly or privately? I loved the sound of the Imam's call, and I was moved by the general reverence during the day, even in the market place; the remembering. My great teacher Frédéric said, 'We must remember, every minute of every hour, of every day, in order to distil our own immortality – and put together all we have known, all we will know and

Turkey

all we know now.' These words were spoken by Hippocrates thousands of years before Christ. This is what these people were doing – remembering. There were many wonders which had to be left unexplored, but like tiny fragments, pieces of what I saw spring to mind, like the wondrous golden coloured mosaic-domed ceilings of what had been a Christian church in Chora, where I sat and gazed at a dome with a picture depicting Jesus healing the sick with his hands. I often remember too, in my mind's eye, the fantastic blue of the Iznik exquisite porcelain and tiles; the dye never to be found again after the sixteenth century.

I returned home to England heavily laden with beautiful reproduction tiles in blues and greens with the symbolic tulip on many of them. The blue was a copy of the famous Iznik blue. What a wonderful place, full of beauty, is Istanbul.

CHAPTER SEVENTEEN

Dark Night of the Soul

Death of Frédéric Lionel – School of Economic Science – East Dean – Prague – Poland

BACK IN THE HEALING CENTRE, the pattern as always was changing, and I once again had the right patients. Many patients were therapists themselves who came to discover and use their own healing powers. With me they gained experience and found support. This was so interesting as all of us seemed to be sowing mustard seeds of knowledge, and many people were benefiting, as in the parable of the mustard seed which I often quote: 'Some seeds fell by the wayside, some grew amongst thorns and perished, some grew fast and died away and some grew a thousand fold.' These were the words which spread and took root. It was an exciting time with all the therapists joining in, and many complementary therapies began to be practised in combination. Openly the doctors began to recognise and revive the original idea of healing which was to combine medicine and healing of the body and soul together.

The Doctor Healer Network, founded many years earlier by an American psychiatrist, now began to enlarge and spread. It had been easier for an outsider to work as a catalyst, and he came to London to do this.

By now, I had completed the videos and was showing them to interested people, so they were very useful. Whenever even now I listen to Frédéric Lionel's tapes, I am inspired and hear something new. He said, 'Healing is the highest form of Man's endeavour.' In 1999, Frédéric became much older – deaf and almost blind, but completely aware of what was going on and in touch with other vibrations. There was a very potent solar eclipse in the August of 1999, when it seemed as if the energy vibrations were being switched to a different channel. I felt this was a portent, the beginning of the New Millennium – a big change was happening. At the beginning of December there was a spectacular and awesome full moon – a bigger moon than had ever been seen. This was a cosmic change and inevitably would bring change to people's lives. At this time in Paris,

Frédéric died. His words are as relevant now as when they were spoken, and all his teaching is most necessary for those who hear it in today's social and ecological climate, and to those who wish to know why they are here.

I was able to delegate most of the management at Uppark to a son-in-law who was always a tower of strength and a vital spoke in the wheel of life there. Uppark was a trust left by Richard that I felt the whole team could now be trusted with, and the remarkable co-ordination between the families was now in action. I felt I had accomplished what I had set out to do there. There had been splendid occasions through the years – twenty-first birthdays, weddings, silver weddings, christenings, big parties, small parties and much laughter and fun, but I felt it was time to become the older generation.

I became very tired and the pollution from aircraft became serious in Barnes. All I had felt ecologically about poisoning the earth and water was happening, and still too few people seemed to be aware of this. The greed for materialism and money blotted out awareness of nature. I got pneumonia and was very ill. It was a terrible shock for the first time in my life to realise I was no longer in control of my life nor my body. This was a testing time, like others before, of my faith and acceptance of my fate, whatever it would be. I recovered, but I was defeated and could no longer go on with the healing clinic and life in London. As the Sufis say, one should learn to die before you die. My family spent more time with their business in the country than in London, so I decided to move to the country and be near them all and watch the smallest grandchildren grow up.

Before I could really make the break (especially from my garden as spring was in the air and the plants were starting to come out), I decided on one more year in London, so I joined a philosophy course at the School of Economic Science. This was one of the most interesting learning experiences I have ever had. It was a wonderfully well-organised course run by very special tutors in Queens Gate. I arrived, the new girl at school, and the oldest person there. This school had been advertised widely, even in the Underground, and therefore comprised people from all walks of life – I loved being with them all. I loved the buzz and the constant interest. Among the students was a cab driver, a publican, an artist, a puppet theatre manager, a mime artist, a missionary and some smartly dressed ladies, wives of high-flying business executives. Some people had done the course before. There was a man who was in love with his dog, which had died, and many others. The tutor was very skilful. Although he had a framework, it didn't appear so, and he managed to keep discussions within a certain wide limit and to keep them off any specific religion or political belief which could digress, but in spite of this everyone was free to ask all manner of questions and receive all manner of answers. He would make one or two remarks and give short readings and ask questions which provoked discussions and answers leading to further thought. This surely was real philosophy as practised by the Greeks in ancient times. The word God was avoided. When I pointed this out, the tutor explained the better word universally accepted was 'consciousness'. It dawned on me after one or two classes that the short silent breaks he introduced were the introduction to meditation. After a few months, this exercise of stillness intensified, and eventually was recognised as meditation. Quite rightly, the word meditation was not mentioned in the original information as knowing and recognising the fear in most people's minds it was felt better to get them interested in the subject of philosophy without further explanation. The meditation taught was of the oldest known method handed down through a line of Indian gurus for hundreds of generations, originally in the Vedic teaching. This school of Indian teachers was referred to by the tutors in the college, and their spiritual grounding, which was obviously so secure, came from there. They used to go and check with their teacher in India. Philosophy was a new world to me – it opened up channels of thought one could pursue and work on all the time. I felt I was coming to life again, on a new wavelength – I began to hear things differently; answers seemed to materialise to long sought after questions. All the time everyone in the class contributed. It was fascinating to hear so many different interpretations of one thought from so many people. Here again the tutor was remarkable in his summing up. The discussions were endless, and some of us used to continue long into the day after the class. I found so much of this philosophy tied up with Frédéric Lionel's wisdom and his writings and sayings. Of course it would, because we are all universal and of one cosmos, but it takes work on oneself to realise this. It was good year and my only regret leaving London was that I could not continue with this course, but I had decided upon a move and no-one can have everything. I felt the benefit of family and country outweighed London.

It almost felt as if big hands were pushing me out of a place where I had both physically and emotionally finished. I felt propelled to the country towards space, I think I needed to look at vast distances. Thus

I found myself driving around the country, within reasonable distance of Uppark and the sea, with my dowsing rods, looking for a house. I visited twenty-two places, dowsing for right earth energy, before I decided on a particular village; I do not know why, for I was proved wrong, except I was not well, so that my dowsing may not have been true. What I did not do was consult an astrologer, which I have done all my life. It has helped me greatly to understand my own particular map of the stars – comparable to watching nature's weather forecast. One can either take shelter from the storm or go out to meet it. Astrology has also helped me to make the momentous decisions in life, which cannot be made for oneself and are better considered when the map of the heavens can be consulted to ensure the truly best outcome. Meeting another astrologer later of great depth, David Bergin, has enabled me through his charts to understand and explain why certain mysteries and situations happened. Life is interesting, and one thing we can all be quite sure of is change.

Searching for a home, I was impatient as always, which made me overlook certain inner subtle signals I was given and chose to ignore. Through what seemed like chance, in a garden magazine I never normally read, I saw an advert for a cottage to let in East Dean, which had charm, and where my dowsing had already led me. I was drawn by the Downs which had sheep, taking me back to thoughts of childhood. I overlooked the fact that looking up from a narrow valley is not the same as looking down. According to Feng Shui, the energy was blocked to my house. I also had a warning experience. The vendor lived next door and had a large garden which had been his wife's pride and joy before she died young. He suggested I would like to sit there before returning to London. It was a beautiful sunny day and I could have another look at my prospective house next door. He left for his office. As I was sitting there in his garden I clearly saw a dark-haired woman who stood over me. She was very forceful and seemingly angry, and said, 'Get out of here, don't come near, go away.' I was shocked and in retrospect misunderstood her. I immediately thought, she doesn't want me near her husband or in her garden. I had to recover, and went and sat in the garden I was planning to buy which felt quite all right – in fact I checked with my dowsing – but I was shaken and was to learn a lesson in delusion. How often we delude ourselves, just to please ourselves.

The house at East Dean was very old and I made a ravishing garden – when I moved into the house at first I thought there was an inquisitive presence which hovered, and I wanted to clear out, so in my way I did this. I think one can help these left over or unfinished presences by offering them assurance, peace, acceptance of what has been, and praying they can let go and move on so they can finally tune in to a higher vibration into which I believe we move. And this happened. It was a pretty house, and it was the garden that really captivated me, but I was not well. It was as if all my energy was being drained. I was fading away and I became very depressed. In fact after a year or two, I went through the dark night of the soul. Life here had started well and I often saw my two smallest grandchildren after nearby school, but they grew up and went off. The family were within range but not that near. I tried to interest people in the village in a healing centre, but there was no enthusiasm. It was a sad village in a time warp, that had no centre. The post office was fast fading, no longer the centre for news and views and gossip, nor a food store. The garage closed down, the pub was uninteresting. Many of the inhabitants' families had lived there for hundreds of years, and nothing seemed to have moved, but age had taken over and the village had lost its heart.

Also, many seemed terribly afraid of what they called New Age things; many of them were Methodist, Baptist, Plymouth Brethren and very strict. Strange, in such a small village with all sorts of different religions, that many wanted nothing to do with anything new.

After a while I went on two short travels to have a change. I went to Prague, but this too was sad. I found Prague beautiful, unkempt and dusty, in the aftermath of communism, the people too indoctrinated to be interesting. They stuck by the guide book and by what they had been told to say. They had no freedom of thought. The food was awful, mostly German dumplings that they had learned about during the occupation. It all seemed rather deadened and soulless. This was utterly different from Poland, where I went two years later. Since nursing the Poles in the war, I had always wanted to see their country; now was my chance – the Iron Curtain down, travel was unrestricted. I travelled with a small group to Krakow and Warsaw. It's always a bit nerve-wracking to meet the other ten people with whom one will be sharing for many days. I arrived at the airport suitably dressed I felt for cold, heat and most eventualities, to see to my horror two grand looking ladies with white gloves, one with a hat on. It was such an unexpected sight, I turned away to collect myself, take a deep breath and prepare again to turn around and meet them. The group had formed before it began. Mercifully I knew some of them but it was very elitist. For the two or three who did not know the others, it was like being at college, where elitism flourished. However, off we set.

Poland was all I had imagined – also dusty, a bit sad, shops empty of luxury food and household goods, the hotels tatty and untouched for years, but underneath it all I could detect and feel the real spirit of the Poles. I knew of their immense courage and bravery against all odds, and deep spiritual centres which had remained unchanged. Music and art was reviving, even among the young, whose parents had secretly withstood communism and had practised their religion. I was most fortunate having several Polish friends, with whom I spent happy evenings. They were so strong in their spiritual faith, and here too it showed in all they were doing and working at, and in their great generosity. In spite of immense difficulty, the Poles were generous to an embarrassing degree. One young man offered me a bowl of fruit containing bananas. Little did I know this was probably a week's wages. He told me he had never seen a banana until the fall of the Iron Curtain. We forget what we have got, and are so busy acquiring what we have not got, we overlook the relative value of THINGS. We were taken to see some very beautiful treasures, which had been hidden during the occupation and recently restored to their

Poland – Cracow

proper place, including precious pictures in private collections. Enjoyable and horrifying expeditions were organised into the country – enjoyable because of the peasant food and vodka, and horrifying to pass mile after mile of completely black trees and houses, polluted by the Russian industrial installations which had devastated not only the land but the people too. To hear Polish music, a concert of Dvorák, played by a Polish orchestra, was the jewel in the crown of musical experiences. It was like hearing the Russians play music which soared above all earthly things to another level, and could be described as being at soul level.

We were entertained one day to tea by Count and Countess Rostwo-rowka in his palace in the middle of Krakow. It was a ruin after the war, and then the Russian occupation, but he was restoring it to its original condition when it had been decorated in the eighteenth century. The Count had no money, but being a sculptor and architect was doing much of the work himself. At the time of the tea-party he had completed two rooms in which they were living. The wallpaper and decorations had been dated to the same period as those at Uppark, so we had much in common. Tea was served in this exquisite drawing room with flock wallpaper and two beautiful silk covered gold chairs, but also several wooden pub folding chairs and a wooden trestle table covered in a damask tablecloth. Tea was poured from a silver teapot on a silver tray into cups and saucers, one or two of which were Meissen, the others were everyday china and mugs. The Count and Countess had rented the downstairs of the palace to Chanel as a boutique for wealthy tourists. It was impressive to witness their courage as they restored what had been such a beautiful cultural masterpiece to its original form using the few remaining precious things which had survived so much. I am sure they will now finish restoring this wonderful home, where they will entertain many people. The tea-party achieved a remarkable air of civilised culture in spite of such misfortune. I bade farewell to Poland with sadness, because though the restoration of some of their palaces was beautiful, it seemed to have little practical future. The Poles have never seemed to me to be practical. They seem to be more aesthetic people, with such big hearts.

CHAPTER EIGHTEEN

Retirement

East Dean – St Roc Healing Centre – David Tredinnick MP – end of refurbishment at Uppark – Upark organic farm – grandchildren – move to West Wittering

T HE FIVE YEARS IN EAST DEAN had been strange – it was a strange place which, when I had a team of dowsers work out the energy lines some years later, proved to be a very negative place. Negative ley lines ran in several strands through the house and garden, carrying along in the water many pollutants, possibly radioactive and detrimental to health. There were underground springs in unexpected places. This water was not pure and clear any more. Several people in the area had died before they were old of cancer – I should have realised, and had overlooked inner signals in order to have what I wanted then and there. I was punished. When I had arrived in East Dean, full of expectation, there seemed to have been a chain of small miracles. I thought the St Roc Healing Centre could be established. I found a fourteenth-century statue of St Roc in a neighbour's garden. I learned that on top of the hill at Goodwood, only a few miles away, were the ruins of a Roman fortress under which were reputed to be the remains of St Roc's chapel. There was a statue of St Roc in the village church and I partook in an annual festival, which was a pilgrimage to St Roc's hill for a healing service on St Roc's anniversary in August. This was a great gathering, and for three years running it was held on utterly beautiful evenings with spectacular sunsets. It was good to see hundreds of people, and lots of them children make the procession from the church in the valley up the very steep hill to a healing service at the top.

One year, Donald Reeves of the St Roc Trust and St James's Piccadilly, came to preach. To see three clerics in long black and white cloaks with lighted braziers standing against the sunset looked medieval, as if from a foreign land far east of England. In spite of all these events, things did not feel right. I felt as if my soul had cracked, and I had lost my motive in life – we cannot go back, we can only go forward and have to be in the now. It seemed the only thing to hold on to – now. Frédéric's wise words came to me – to spend every hour of every day distilling our immortality. We must learn to accept the unacceptable and then we are free. So onwards: I kept feeling that I wanted to go to the sea – whenever I felt suffocated by events or the house, I had this urge for the sea. I was missing my annual winter retreats in Spain which I had enjoyed for many years, so I often drove to the sea at West Wittering where I temporarily recovered, after staring into space and light.

One good thing happened while I was in East Dean which got me going. I was introduced to a young politician called David Tredinnick MP. For twelve years he has been treasurer of the Parliamentary Group for Complementary and Alternative Medicine, and he wanted to know more about healing. Here was someone on my wavelength, with a brilliant intellect, and an academic approach to things which I had always known about instinctively and intuitively, but lacked the ability to put together in a practical way. He understood both sides of the card. David and I have had many dialogues and discussions through the years, covering subjects including the Tarot, alchemy, astrology, ecological issues, organic living and many more. Each meeting led us on to more searching for knowledge – his questions inspired me to action once more, and I found myself having to revise writings and notes from years before to find the answers. He plied me with interesting new books about old subjects written in what I considered a new quick-fix way. I found it hard to accept that anyone could become an alchemist by reading a book on the subject and doing some exercises. I was quite shocked by this, but it was an insight into what was going on amongst new, young thinkers and seekers – and I was refreshed and felt revived by being in touch with events. Without David this book would never have been completed, but he encouraged me to go on and pushed me over the last fence. To him I owe thanks.

It was time I realised a new world. I was grateful for the chance to enter it and to be aware of what was going on. David's healing developed as time went on, from starting secretly with a toe in the water. After a few years he became a powerful healer and a splendid political representative of the present day way to enlightenment. Many people are ready to move into a state of higher awareness and do healing, but need the support to give them courage – it is fear which holds us back. I observe a fashionable practice called Reiki going on. Anyone can pay to learn this and practise it for money. It is acceptable because it has a name, a certificate, a training and can be bought and paid for. It works, in many cases, because the people who practise it are healers anyway and rightly motivated. Again, I find it hard to accept that compassion, healing and love should be treated as a commodity. In the past I helped many therapists start consciously healing to enhance what they were already practising – better, I felt it could add another dimension to a profession, and to one's own knowledge.

The light from the sea drew me nearer the coast, until I finally moved to live in West Wittering. I have never been a believer in going back to places where I have been before until now. A place, like a person, is an experience to have, to hold, to pass on. I do not believe one should hold on, but I had to return for an interim period to the house at Uppark. After the fire I had let go of Uppark in my feelings, but there was something unfinished. Sarah was around in essence and it was as if she was still hovering about to see what would happen. I moved back to Uppark for a few months, until the house I was buying in West Wittering was ready. Strange that the day I got back to Uppark I had a heart attack. This too, was an interesting experience, because I realised I was absolutely ready to go on elsewhere, and my only worries were for entirely practical reasons. But anyway I recovered. Perhaps illness was just as well, as my thoughts could only be concentrated towards myself, not on any sentiments about past events nor the house. Having rested a while I felt I and the house became reconciled, and Sarah ceased walking around and was no longer restless, nor even there for me. She had transferred her care to the family. They were beginning to live there again. It was reviving in a new way; refurbished by my daughters and adjusting to new life yet retaining its basic beauty and grace. The next two generations were growing and filling it up with people, parties, festivals. My daughters were sharing their good fortune with others, and many charity benefit events took place. Life was positive and circulating goodwill around.

I longed to finish the necklace of my life, and be by the sea. I had done what I had set out to do at Uppark which was to keep it all going until my three daughters were established in their lives, and I could see they most certainly were. Now I intended to retire. In 2001 to my intense joy the farm at Uppark received organic farming recognition, which I had first wished in 1949 when Sir George Trevelyan and Lady Eve Balfour had visited. It had been a cry in the wilderness then, and here and now the cry was being heard everywhere. To my equal joy I find that some

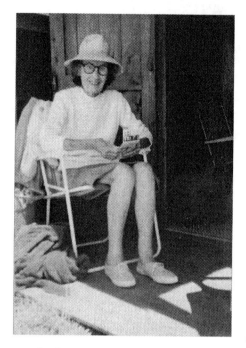

Retirement, West Wittering

of my grandchildren have healing hands like my daughters and this they will use for the benefit of others in a modern way. So my wishes have come true – they do. I see more beads – of different colours – for another necklace in the future.

Here in West Wittering, I find that this is not only a place of good and powerful energy, but also a place of an awesome light which affects people. This light energy seems to be in everything, in all kinds of little miracles, that led me on my search to houses for sale; something would deflect me if it was not right. After a prolonged search and various false starts, I bought the first house I had been drawn to many months before. I could have trusted my instincts, but I had been unnerved by my East Dean experience. My dowsing was right this time and I bought it. Here I am in wonderful light and sun, with flowers surrounding me and near the sea which I can hear all the time. And here I hope to stay in a wonderful stillness and great peace. And when the next handful of beads comes along, I shall see what happens.

Epilogue

SINCE FINISHING THIS BOOK many of those mentioned have died, retired or moved on to other environments.

John Petty retired from Coventry, and Donald Reeves is engaged in a reconciliation project in Bosnia called 'Soul of Europe'.

My whole family, two generations of them, are all aware of a new conciousness and a different way of living life in tune with the infinite. They contribute through creating as painters, designers, master chefs, sculptors, ecologically friendly agriculturalists, business and charity work, and above all, healing.

The main thread throughout is communication and free discussion on all levels on subjects as varied as philosophy, religion, fashion, herbs, healing and quantum physics. Long may it continue and may the mustard seeds of knowledge be scattered and flourish.